Women and Leadership

Essential Skills for Success in Today's Business

Edited by National Press Publications

NATIONAL PRESS PUBLICATIONS

A Division of Rockhurst University Continuing Education Center, Inc.

6901 West 63rd Street • P.O. Box 2949 • Shawnee Mission, Kansas 66201-1349

1-800-258-7248 • 1-913-432-7757

Women and Leadership: Essential Skills for Success in Today's Business

Published by National Press Publications, Inc.
Copyright 2000 National Press Publications, Inc.
A Division of Rockhurst University Continuing Education Center, Inc.

Printed in the United States of America

1 2 3 4 5 6 7 8 9 10

ISBN 1-55852-282-4

Table of Contents

1 ARE YOU READY FOR LEADERSHIP?

Are You Ready for Leadership?

- Not everyone who is a leader now is doing as good a job as she'd like to do.

- Not everyone has skills in every area of leadership.

- Not everyone is confident and relaxed in her leadership role.

- Not everyone knows what to do with the power that comes with leadership.

- Not everyone is able to strike a balance between her personal and professional lives.

- Not everyone knows her own leadership abilities.

But everyone has the potential for leadership. And in today's workplace, more leadership opportunities are available to more women than ever before — if they are ready for them.

The Workplace of the 21st Century Will Be Different

Prepare yourself for the future. Here are 26 situations to be expected by managers of this new century:

1. Unimaginably fast information systems

2. Instant access to the global marketplace

3. "Virtual" everything — teams, offices, organizations

4. Management of workers who are present plus workers who are not

5. Teams with members who come together physically and with members from around the world

6. Even less job stability

7. More outsourcing

8. Freelance, contract work

9. Specialization

10. Technology

11. Loose job descriptions

12. Moving and relocating often

13. Fewer, larger global corporations

14. Lots of decentralization

15. Fewer workers

16. Interest in workplace ethics, fairness, balance

17. Less structured working hours

18. Working from home

19. Individual responsibility for own career, own pension, insurance, etc.

20. Half a day each day to come up to speed on changes and new information

21. Creativity vital to the job

22. Stable personality more valued than knowledge or skills

23. Harder on counterproductive behavior like absenteeism

24. Getting and giving coaching

25. Less charismatic leadership and more substance, authenticity, people skills

26. Psychological consulting for personality assessments and team-building

Facing New Values, Roles and Work Forms

In addition, leaders today must face new and challenging values, roles and work forms:

New Values: Sharing information fully with the team, rather than the old style of "need to know" communication. Involving staff in the areas of decision-making, goal-setting and planning. Empowering people by listening, coaching, mentoring and counseling. Welcoming a diversity of viewpoints. Encouraging risk-taking and creativity. Expecting change.

New, Multiple Roles: No longer using the old model of autocratic management but, rather, seeking democratic leadership with a focus on multiple roles. Leaders are expected to be coaches, counselors, mentors, trainers, delegators, team leaders, problem-solvers, goal-setters, innovators and communicators. Each role is interdependent and each role involves interaction with peers and employees. Leadership is by influence rather than by command.

New Work Forms: An emphasis on the team concept, with participation in work teams, task forces and cross-functional teams, as well as the encouragement of self-directed teams.

Are You Ready to Face These Challenges?

The skills of leadership today rely heavily on personal power and effective influence with others, yet many women find these two areas particularly difficult to master. We are products of our time, our culture and our society — all of which still hold the image of the leader to be a male image. The majority of leadership positions are still filled by males, the male pattern of dress is considered the only appropriate dress for formal business, and the deeper voice, taller physique and aggressive posture of the male is seen as necessary to be an effective leader.

Although you may not agree with these perceptions of leadership, it's important to recognize that they exist in our society, if not consciously, then on a subconscious level. Therefore, as a woman, any behavior that you exhibit will be assessed on this same subconscious level against the male image of leadership. If your behavior does not meet this image, you are immediately stereotyped as lacking in leadership potential.

Consider some of the self-limiting behaviors that you may be exhibiting which are judged on this subconscious level. How often have you reacted in a situation, and afterwards said to yourself, "Why do I always do that?"

You don't want to use that particular mode of behavior. You know it is self-limiting. You know it is ineffective. Yet, time and again, that's the behavior that you use. In effect, you are exchanging positive leadership behaviors for self-limiting behaviors. This can be disastrous for your career. You may not be promoted any further, because your future potential is dependent upon how you are perceived in your present position in terms of your effectiveness as a leader and manager.

Meet six women who exhibit self-limiting behaviors.

1. Marlene is the department manager of quality control. She's a high achiever and a hard worker. People know that if you give Marlene a project, it gets done and gets done right! The i's are dotted and the t's are crossed. That's why Marlene got promoted — because she did such exceptional work.

   Now, as department manager, Marlene still does most of the work. She gives her subordinates small, insignificant projects, and checks and rechecks everything they do. In fact, she often takes back the work she gives them, saying, "If I want it done right, I might as well do it myself."

   Marlene is most comfortable when there are standard operating procedures to follow. She thinks the rules and formal channels are the way to do things correctly. She is wary of change and encourages her group to do things the way they've always been done.

   In fact, when the new computer system was introduced, it caused her stress, anger and frustration because she didn't know how to operate it. Rather than admit this and ask for training, she stayed late every night and eventually mastered the system — her way. And that's how she expects her group to use it — her way. She resents any suggestion that there is a better way to operate the programs or that her group might benefit from training from computer support.

   Marlene is stressed and angry. She feels overworked and underappreciated. She thinks, "If they'd just do things the 'right' way, we wouldn't have all these problems."

How do Marlene's behaviors affect her leadership effectiveness?

Marlene's group suffers from low morale, low productivity, lack of creativity and initiative and stress. They have little opportunity to learn new skills, improve their current skill base or develop their potential for promotion.

Marlene's self-limiting behaviors say that in all things she must be perfect.

2. Pat is the manager of the training department of a large company. Most of the time, she feels tense and overloaded. The marketing department requested a new series of programs, and although Pat knew the training calendar was already full, she agreed to add the programs. Now, she has to find time to plan the programs, as well as allocate this extra work to her staff. She wants to have a congenial team and does all she can to make everyone feel part of the group. She plans to bring donuts and coffee to the planning meeting, hoping that her team will appreciate the gesture.

    At the meeting, she tries to let them know diplomatically that there will be a lot of extra work in the next few weeks. She doesn't want to come right out and tell them what she has promised to the marketing department in case her staff members are angry with her commitment of their time and effort. She wonders how she can get her one problematic staff member on her side, since when he is unhappy, he seems to get everyone else against her as well. She has been meaning to speak to him about his negative attitude but doesn't want to upset him further.

    Pat thinks that a reward system — perhaps a special cake at the next meeting — might motivate them to do the work. She feels frustrated with her inability to get everyone working on the same side. She hates it when her staff members are flippant or cold toward her.

Pat's overcommitment brings stress and anger to everyone. Staff feel that they aren't consulted and aren't part of a team. They also know that they can manipulate Pat by withholding their approval of her. Unfortunately, since Pat is seldom direct with them, they often misunderstand her directions and performance deteriorates.

Pat's underlying behaviors are an attempt to please everyone.

3. Gloria is one of the most effective systems analysts that the company ever hired. Gloria knows computers inside and out. She can solve the most complex problems, troubleshoot for every situation, and repair highly detailed programming errors. When she was a specialist in the systems support group, she could be counted on to find the solutions to whatever problems the rest of the organization might have. That's why she was promoted to manager of the group.

   Gloria hates her new position. She hates having to deal with people all day, especially her peers in other departments. She doesn't care what their responsibilities are or how the departments interact. She just wants them to give her the problem, leave her alone and let her get on with the job. And she tells them so.

   Gloria is frustrated with being "out of the line of fire." She often keeps the more interesting problems for herself, telling herself she's just "keeping up her skills." Sometimes, this means that she doesn't have time to deal with the day-to-day managerial issues of paperwork, personnel performance appraisal and conflict resolution. In fact, she doesn't see why her group can't just do their jobs and leave her alone to do hers.

Gloria's group is frustrated with the lack of leadership and communication from Gloria. They don't know what goals are set for the department, what projects are coming up, who is assigned to what task, whether their performance is adequate, or how their interpersonal conflicts are going to be resolved. Morale is low and performance is rapidly deteriorating.

Gloria's behaviors say that she is unable to let go of her specialist/detail perspective, a common issue when a person is promoted from a "doer" position to a "manager" position.

4. Carmen is manager of the customer service department. She is conscientious in her work, good with her people, and enjoys the interaction with the public. Recently, she was confronted with an angry customer who wanted immediate satisfaction on his complaint. Carmen knew that he was a regular customer of her company with a sizable account. However, she didn't feel that she had the authority to do anything without her boss's permission. Unfortunately, her boss was away on a weeklong training course and couldn't be reached.

    This has happened to Carmen before. Once, her boss left her with a project to do while he attended an overnight business meeting, but the details were not specified. Carmen was reluctant to begin until her boss spelled out exactly what he expected from her and, as a result, left the project until his return.

    Carmen would like to try some new call procedures that will speed up the system but is still waiting for approval to go ahead. Her proposal seems to be tied up on someone's desk, but she's not sure who has it. She doesn't feel it's her place to go after the approval — that's her boss's job.

Carmen's behaviors don't adversely affect her group, but they will affect her own performance appraisals. She'll be seen as a nonself-starter, lacking in initiative, unable to carry work through independently, and ineffective in situations calling for creative solutions.

Carmen exhibits the behaviors of a person who lacks self-confidence, someone who needs "permission" before doing anything outside the rules and regulations.

5. Shirelle manages the administrative support group with 23 people reporting to her. Sometimes, Shirelle thinks they are 23 people who all hate one another. She seems to spend most of her time tiptoeing around conflict, avoiding arguments, playing political games, trying to smooth over hurt feelings, keeping certain parties apart and listening to everyone's gripes and whines. She keeps hoping that things will calm down, but they just seem to be getting worse.

   Shirelle feels like she's sitting on a time bomb, and she hates the feeling of tension and anger in the department. She's afraid to say anything to anyone for fear of being seen as "taking sides." So, she tends to go into her office and shut the door to avoid dealing with the conflicts that keep arising in the group.

How do Shirelle's behaviors affect her team? Her team is divided into two opposing camps with people choosing sides. They speak of "us" and "them," and angry words often break out. There's a lot of gossip and backbiting, morale is low and absenteeism abounds.

Shirelle thinks that conflict is negative, and her behaviors indicate that she tries to avoid conflict at all costs.

6. Margaret has been the administrative assistant to the director of the company for the past 10 years. She does her job exceptionally well and is frustrated that she has never been promoted to a management position. She thinks her boss should know how well she does her job and should recognize her skills and abilities without her having to tell him.

   Margaret feels uncomfortable with "pushing herself forward" and is silent in most meetings, even when she has an opinion she'd like to state. On the few occasions when she does speak, she feels she is discounted because she's not a manager.

   She also suspects that being a woman works against her, and she often feels at a disadvantage with her male peers. Once, she had to supervise a young intern, who was also male, and found it difficult to stay away from the "mother" role.

She'd like to be in management in her company but has no idea of how to go about climbing the corporate ladder.

Margaret's low profile might be safe, but it also locks her out of being seen as a "go-getter." She misses a lot of opportunities to show what she can do.

Her behaviors suggest a lack of self-confidence and credibility as a woman.

When the behaviors of these women are put up against the image of effective leadership, these women are seen as lacking in leadership abilities and skills. In fact, they are no more lacking in abilities than men are in the same circumstances, but our society's subconscious image of leadership as a male prerogative put the women at a disadvantage.

The only way to combat this is to recognize your own self-limiting behaviors and eliminate them by giving yourself permission to change and adapt new, positive behaviors.

Do You Exhibit Any of These Self-Limiting Behaviors?

- Are you a perfectionist, determined to do everything "right"?

- Do you try to please everyone so that they will like you?

- Are you stuck on your specialist skill level, finding it difficult to move to people skills?

- Are you reluctant to take the initiative in situations where you don't have specific permission to go beyond your perceived authority?

- Do you try to avoid conflict?

- Are you uncomfortable with self-promotion?

Check the following questions that ring somewhat true with you. Do them quickly without making deep judgments.

_____ 1. Do you have trouble assigning important projects to subordinates?

_____ 2. Do you think your subordinate won't complete an assignment as well as you would?

_____ 3. Do you have trouble asking for assistance?

_____ 4. Do you oversupervise as opposed to undersupervise your subordinates?

_____ 5. Do you prefer a "rule-to-follow" approach to doing your work?

_____ 6. Do you hate trying things that you've never done before?

_____ 7. Do you feel overextended at work?

_____ 8. Do you make promises or commitments that you can't meet?

_____ 9. Do you have trouble saying "no"?

Reflections

_____ 10. Do you have trouble dealing with problem subordinates?

_____ 11. Do you find yourself needing your subordinates to like you?

_____ 12. Do you make decisions based on how your subordinates will react?

_____ 13. Do you prefer the technical parts of your job over the managing parts?

_____ 14. Do you dislike having to deal with people problems?

_____ 15. Do you feel the need to be left alone to get work done?

_____ 16. Do you understand how your department functions but not how the total company competes or works in the marketplace?

_____ 17. Do you prefer working on projects alone rather than overseeing others doing the projects?

_____ 18. Do you allow others to do the goal-setting and visioning for your department?

_____ 19. Do you often wait for your boss to give you directions?

_____ 20. Do you feel uncomfortable doing something that isn't directly under your job description?

_____ 21. Do you put off going ahead with an idea until you have approval?

_____ 22. Do you like things spelled out precisely with plenty of feedback?

_____ 23. Do you wait for your boss to set goals for your department?

_____ 24. Do you expect your boss to make decisions about your career?

Reflections

_____ 25. Do you see conflict as negative?

_____ 26. Do you prefer to keep out of arguments, even when you are right?

_____ 27. Do you avoid dealing with difficult people?

_____ 28. Do you try to ignore the gossiping in your department?

_____ 29. Do you feel as if you are working in an armed camp?

_____ 30. Do you avoid situations in which there might be anger or tears?

_____ 31. Do you dislike high visibility in the organization?

_____ 32. Do you dislike "tooting your own horn" to your boss when you accomplish a tough project?

_____ 33. Do you dislike having to play politics to get ahead?

_____ 34. Does the word "power" have negative connotations for you?

_____ 35. Does supervising a male create images of a problem situation?

_____ 36. Do you feel discounted when you participate in groups made up mostly of males at a meeting?

Reflections

Reflections

Scoring

If you checked:

Questions 1-6: You may have some self-limiting behaviors of perfectionism.

Questions 7-12: You may be trying to please others with your behaviors.

Questions 13-18: You may be stuck in the technical phase of your career, with behaviors that show a reluctance to learn people skills.

Questions 19-24: You may be avoiding conflict or dealing with confrontational situations.

Questions 25-30: Your behaviors may be showing a lack of initiative or self-confidence.

Questions 31-36: You may be exhibiting self-deprecating behaviors.

Reflections

2 THE FUNCTION OF LEADING

What is "leading"? Leadership is defined as the function of one who guides or directs a group. There are no leaders without followers.

Leadership is the most important managerial function you'll learn, because it's through people that goals and objectives are accomplished. The way you manage or lead your employees determines the degree of success your unit, division and total organization will have.

Leadership is knowing your subordinates and what motivates them. It's knowing the motivating characteristics of jobs, tasks and projects. It's knowing the group dynamics of your work unit. It's the ability to lead, plan, direct, organize, inspire, motivate, learn, teach, train, resolve conflicts, build an effective team and keep performance high.

Sounds a little like being part superwoman and part genius, doesn't it?

What Do Leaders Do?

A leader is someone who plans, organizes, controls, communicates, delegates, coaches and accepts responsibility for reaching the organization's goals. A leader has the authority and responsibility to accomplish the goals of her unit and is held accountable for results. A leader is also a manager.

What Don't Leaders Do?

Leaders are active. They do not:

- Sit around waiting for others to act

- Hope someone is there, following along

- Go it alone

- Fail to communicate where they are headed and what is to be done

- Leave their group milling about with no directions

Developing Your Leadership Style

Your leadership style is the way in which you function and relate to people at all levels within the company. This style is a direct result of your personal philosophy regarding those who work for you.

> Ann believes that the seven people in her department must be closely supervised at all times to ensure that they do the work assigned to them. Otherwise, they will slack off and waste time talking and socializing. She thinks that they are uninterested in the overall goals and objectives of the department and have no desire to contribute to the setting of them. She has no faith in their ability to handle responsibility and gives them very little opportunity to work independently. In fact, she believes that they prefer to simply do the work and collect their paychecks.

If you believe, as Ann does, that people have an inherent dislike of work and will try to avoid it whenever possible, that they will only achieve goals and objectives if pushed or punished, and that they don't want responsibility, have little ambition and prefer to be directed, then your leadership style is probably one in which you make the decisions, manage the work and direct others. This is a **directive** leadership style.

Bea thinks that two heads are better than one and six heads better still. She encourages the whole department to brainstorm ideas for improving productivity. She elicits suggestions for innovative changes to procedures. She tries to give her subordinates opportunities to be responsible for aspects of their jobs and encourages them to set their own goals and choose their own work styles.

If like Bea, you're inclined to believe that people can be motivated to excel, want to exercise creativity and self-discipline on the job, seek responsibility and enjoy challenges, then you will probably lead them with an empowerment style that encourages participation and interaction in all aspects of work. This is a **consultative** leadership style.

The Leadership Style for the 21st Century

New types of leaders are emerging in this century. These people tend to lead organizations through the challenges of global competition, deregulation, rapid technological change and a diverse workplace.

Leaders today are seen as facilitators of self-directed teams. They encourage their subordinates to ask questions, state opinions and share information. They facilitate the problem-solving, decision-making, goal-setting and development of the work procedures that teams do.

This is the **facilitative** leadership style.

The Modes of Leadership

In addition to the three styles of leadership, there is also a mode of leadership that you will adapt. The two modes are task and social.

Dorothy is a director in a government agency. She spends much of her time setting the stage for her "leading." She meticulously plans what needs to be done. Her plans interconnect — her daily plans fit into her weekly plans which fit into her monthly plans. The long-range plans and their objectives are given to her by her boss. She breaks this annual plan down into small increments with the milestone-marker approach. What needs to be done by March, by June, by September? Then she knows what needs to be done monthly in order to reach her objectives. After this action plan is set, she knows what to organize, who to organize and how to organize. She makes an appointment to meet with each employee each month. She sets the goals for the month and sets two interim meetings to ensure that the goals are being met. The meetings are formal and businesslike. Other than these meetings, she has very little interaction with her subordinates.

Dorothy is a **task leader**. The work gets done, but her group often feels that she doesn't care about them very much. They see her as distant and cold, more interested in getting the job done than in how they are as individuals.

Molly is the supervisor of a word processing support group. She doesn't do much planning but simply takes the work as it comes in and hands it out. She assumes her subordinates know how to prioritize and organize their individual workloads. She also does a lot of the word processing herself, so she doesn't have a lot of time to check back and review the work flow.

She sees herself as "one of the gang" and enjoys socializing with her group. The weekly staff meetings seldom have an agenda and usually end up being an opportunity to catch up on one another's families and activities. Molly always remembers everyone's birthdays and anniversaries, and the group often enjoys an impromptu party.

Molly is a **social leader**. Molly's group all love her, but they are frustrated by the lack of organization and planning. Often, work gets dumped on someone who is already overloaded. Errors abound, and no one does a quality control check. They'd like more direction and boundaries set by Molly.

Fern, a product manager, does her planning much like Molly. Like Molly, she is comfortable on a social level with her subordinates.

For example, each employee is assigned a set of tasks or a job. Fern meets with each person, and they set mutually agreed-upon objectives. She'll informally chat with them and see how they're doing throughout the week or month. She has an open-door policy, so they can touch base with her anytime.

Fern is a planner, but she also enjoys interaction with her subordinates. Fern is both a **task and social leader**. She uses both leadership styles effectively.

Leaders Are Made, Not Born

Management, leadership and supervisory skills are acquired by those who want to manage. No one is born with the ability to step into a leadership position.

> When Margie was promoted from data entry clerk to supervisor of her group, her boss told her, "You've got what it takes to move ahead in this company. You're definitely management potential."

> Margie wondered exactly what her boss meant. She didn't have any more education or training than the rest of her group. She had worked hard, met deadlines and exhibited initiative. She knew how to get the job done, how to get cooperation from her peers, how to handle difficult people, and how to interact with other managers and supervisors. Were these the characteristics that made her "management potential"?

When you begin to assess the qualities and skills that make an effective leader, certain words come to mind: assertive, flexible, efficient, confident, cooperative, positive, planner, knowledgeable, communicator, initiator, self-starter, controlled, anticipatory, solution-finder, organized, relational, motivating, influential, smart, assessing, realistic and honest. Does anyone have all these qualities and skills? No. We all possess some of them to various degrees. However, it is possible to develop those that you lack. You do this through recognition of your basic strengths, assessment of the areas in which you are weak, and continued self-improvement and self-assessment.

The Key Competencies

The various qualities and skills of a leader can be grouped into four key competencies:

1. Self-Management Skills

   - Professional image

   - Personal assertiveness

2. People Skills

   - Written and oral communication

   - Empowerment of others

   - Motivation of others

   - Conflict resolution

   - Team-building

   - Any other skills that relate to the direct supervision/leadership of others, such as performance appraisal, discipline and delegation

3. Planning Skills

   - Goal-setting and visioning

   - Planning and organization

   - Creativity

   - Problem-solving

   - Logic

   - Conceptual skills

4. Implementation Skills

- System knowledge

- Political savvy

- Practicality

- Flexibility

- Enthusiasm

- Agent for change

What Kind of Leader Are You?

For each statement, rate yourself from 1 to 5, with 1 being "very much like me" or "strongly agree," to 5 being "not at all like me" or "strongly disagree."

_____ 1. If I have to set goals for my group, I do it myself. I know what needs to be done and who can do it.

_____ 2. I am a good problem-solver and prefer to take care of most issues that arise in our group.

_____ 3. I don't have any difficulty in directing others in what they need to do. I lay things out very specifically for them.

_____ 4. If I have to get something done, I will use my authority to do so.

_____ 5. Sometimes, I have to crack the whip in order to get people to do their jobs.

_____ 6. I have a structured plan of action that is specific and well-thought-out.

_____ 7. If I want ideas from my subordinates, I can ask them. I don't appreciate being given a lot of ideas that aren't called for in what we are currently doing.

_____ 8. If a subordinate doesn't like something I'm doing, that's the subordinate's issue, not mine.

_____ 9. I am comfortable taking all the credit for what my department accomplishes. After all, that's my job.

Reflections

_____ 10. An employee's personal problems should be left at home where they belong.

_____ 11. The average manager is not paid to provide counseling to employees. That's the job of specialists in the human resources department.

_____ 12. I believe that my skills on the job do make me an expert in my department.

_____ 13. The feedback process is taken care of through structured employee-appraisal systems. I don't think it's necessary to continually tell employees how they're doing.

_____ 14. If you are in management, you should have some privileges such as parking spaces, bigger offices, special training events, etc.

_____ 15. If subordinates listened more closely to instructions, we wouldn't have so many errors in our systems.

Add up your total score.

- 15-25: You tend to be a directive leader in your style.

- 26-50: You tend to be more consultative in your style.

- 51-75: You are most likely a facilitative leader.

Reflections

Your Vision of Yourself as a Leader

1. Write a quick list of five words describing yourself as a leader. Don't think too long. Use words that end in "ing," such as achieving, inspiring, coping, etc.

    *   _____

    *   _____

    *   _____

    *   _____

    *   _____

2. Circle the one word you would really like to use to describe your image and use it in a sentence describing you as the leader.

3. Expand the sentence into a short paragraph that really defines your image. Use descriptions of how you behave in specific situations.

Reflections

3 WOMEN'S PARTICULAR LEADERSHIP STRENGTHS

Margie knew that her co-worker Don had expected to be given the new position. However, Margie's boss told her that the position needed particular skills in people management and teamwork. Like Margie, Don was a hard worker who got things done, but Don had a reputation for being a bit of a loner, someone who was a stickler for protocol and who seldom interacted with the rest of the group.

Carl was also expecting the same promotion. He was already a section leader. Carl ran his section like a commander in chief, overseeing every detail of the work, keeping close tabs on his people and continually pointing out their errors. Although his section had impressive production, the personnel turnover was high and morale was low.

Yet Margie got the promotion!

Do women have any advantages in the leadership arena? Absolutely! Studies have shown that women are less likely than men to use the traditional directive leadership approach. Instead, women favor the consultative style discussed in the previous chapter. They rely on their personal power as opposed to their positional power; they try to align an employee's personal goals with the employee's work goals; they encourage participation and the sharing of power and information; and they enhance the self-worth of others through positive reinforcement and encouragement.

Women will find it easier than men to move to the new facilitative approach to leadership that is being recognized as the style of this century.

The following attributes will give women an edge as leaders:

1. Encouraging participation

Many women are comfortable encouraging the participation of others in many of the business processes. They solicit suggestions and ideas and are not threatened by the participation of their subordinates. In fact, women often invite others to get involved, using a conversational style and an interactive informal forum for discussion.

There are both pros and cons to this kind of participatory style. In some cases, the female leader may be seen as not having the answers, open to influence by others or giving up her control. However, the same style empowers others, motivates those who want to be included, and enables people to cooperate to reach group goals.

2. Sharing power and information

Women are more likely to share information with others rather than rely on a directive style or "need to know" basis of information-sharing. They will explain the reasoning behind their decisions, discuss the ramifications of a strategic plan and solicit feedback from others.

Again, this has both pros and cons. Sharing power and information creates loyalty in others because they feel trusted. It also sets the tone for others to share power and information and expands the communications flow.

The risks of sharing may be that such actions are seen as weak. The leader may be perceived as lacking in authority, and people may resent not having their ideas used by the leader.

3. Enhancing the self-worth of others

This ability is crucial to the facilitative leadership style, and it is an aspect of a woman's style that is a by-product of the first two. Women enhance subordinates' self-worth by treating them as equals, praising them for work well-done, and sending them small signals of recognition such as personal notes and celebration events.

4. Energizing others

Women tend to have an upbeat approach to encouraging others to enjoy and participate in work projects. They are enthusiastic, positive and practical. They can help others focus on the importance of what is being done and show them how every contribution is vital to the whole task.

Women look for ways to motivate others beyond the paycheck and raises. They understand that some are turned-on by challenge, others by fast growth and others by recognition. They try to suit the work to the motivating factor of the worker.

Male/Female Leadership Skills

Many stereotypes still exist between how men and women are perceived in leadership roles. Studies have revealed a set of specific skills that organizations look for in performance evaluations of candidates for top management positions.

Here are the top 10 skills looked for in management candidates:

1. Make certain that employees understand the purpose of the work unit and how it ties in to the organizational mission

2. Show a basic willingness to take charge, to take responsibility, to find out how to get results, to get the job done

3. Follow up to see that customer needs are met

4. Take action before being forced by the situation

5. Determine customer needs and wants that affect the business unit

6. Develop new strategies for meeting customer needs

7. Gear procedures and methods to achieving customer satisfaction

8. Understand the effects of competition in meeting customer needs; be flexible in responding to rapidly changing needs

9. Delegate skillfully and effectively

10. Take calculated business risks

As you can see, none of these skills is particularly masculine or feminine, yet in studies on the need for skill improvement, stereotypes about women managers still prevail. It was perceived that in order to achieve a top management role, women, in general, needed to work on the following skills:

- Maintain emotional control in tense or emotional situations

- Avoid impulsive actions, act thoughtfully and consider consequences

- Make a commitment to reach the top by balancing other commitments accordingly

Women are still seen as emotional, impulsive and lacking in commitment.

Personality Characteristics

What about the personalities of the top leaders? Are there commonalities? According to a study by Sidney Lecker, a New York psychiatrist, highly successful executives and entrepreneurs exhibited particular personality traits. They were:

1. Persistent and undaunted by failure

2. Unafraid of thinking big

3. Able to set simple objectives

4. Able to identify key data and actions to meet objectives

5. Able to carry complex ideas through to completion

6. Able to search for facts and weigh them

7. Able to take calculated risks

8. Able to take total responsibility

9. Lacking guilt or fear about success

10. Loving the seeking, achieving and savoring of success

11. In command of inner resources: intelligence, creativity and emotional strength

Of these characteristics, the most important was to be in command of inner resources.

The Bottom Line for Women in Leadership

In terms of skills, abilities and characteristics, women have as much to offer in the leadership role as men. In some areas, they may even have an edge over men. However, the actual skills, abilities and characteristics are not as important as the ability to use them. By tapping into your inner resources, you can create a wellspring of power to take you into the leadership field.

How Do Your Leadership Skills Measure Up?

Rate your level by circling:

1 — High level of competency/ability

2 — Average level of competency/ability

3 — Low level of competency/ability

	1	2	3
Initiative: The ball is in your court, and you have to make a decision that does not have the approval of your manager.	1	2	3
Self-starter: It's time to put your plans into action, and you need to take the first steps toward achieving the goals.	1	2	3
Control: Tempers flare during your meeting, and you need to maintain emotional control and stay focused on the objectives of the meeting.	1	2	3
Efficiency: Several different projects are in progress and deadlines are looming. How do you meet the challenge?	1	2	3
Communicator: Do your people know what it is they are supposed to do and how you want it done?	1	2	3
Confidence: You can speak out and give your opinions in the management meetings.	1	2	3

Reflections

	1	2	3
Knowledgeable: Your field is changing rapidly, and you need to keep up with all the changes in order to maintain your knowledge level.	1	2	3
Cooperative: You and your peers need to work together in order to achieve mutual goals.	1	2	3
Assertive: You stand up for your opinions and confront others when it is necessary.	1	2	3
Anticipatory: You've made your plans based upon a number of anticipated responses and issues.	1	2	3
Solution-finder: The problems keep cropping up, and you need to find creative solutions to deal with them.	1	2	3
Organized: You have an overall plan for your group, and you know what to expect from them and when.	1	2	3
Motivating: You inspire your group, motivating them to excel at their jobs.	1	2	3
Influential: When you need to, you know how to reach the "power people" in your company.	1	2	3
Smart: The politics of your company are well-known to you. You know how things work and how to make them work for you.	1	2	3
Realistic: You handle both criticism and evaluation well.	1	2	3

Reflections

Reflections

4 PROFESSIONAL IMAGE AND ASSERTIVE STYLE

Stella is the administrative assistant to the art director of a large advertising agency. There is no strict dress code in the organization, and Stella generally wears casual trousers and colorful blouses. In the summer, she opts for sandals and cotton T-shirts.

Stella is required to attend most meetings in the department. She doesn't feel comfortable volunteering any information — even when she knows of details that her boss could use — but waits until she is asked a question. When replying, she usually avoids eye contact, speaks softly and ends with an upward inflection on the last syllable so that she doesn't sound pushy or bold.

When her boss invited her to attend a formal product-announcement event, she didn't think it was worth buying a new business outfit for just that one event, especially since she wouldn't be wearing it again on the job. Instead, she just kept in the background and made sure that the coffeepots were replenished.

Stella can't understand why she is stuck in her job. She knows she's good at what she does, learns quickly and is an asset to her boss. At Stella's last performance appraisal, her boss told her that she couldn't "see her in a management role." Stella isn't sure what she meant by that remark.

The fact is, Stella's boss was really saying that Stella's image wasn't very professional. She didn't "look" like someone who would fit into leadership.

Does this mean that Stella should go out and buy herself a whole new wardrobe for the job? No, not at all. There's more to a professional image than just the clothes you wear.

A professional image is made up of many factors:

- Poise

- Self-confidence

- Dress

- Posture

- Voice

- Speech patterns

- Body language

We discussed the issues of self-limiting behaviors in the first chapter of this book. When you learn to identify and deal with these behaviors that hold you back from leadership, you'll become more self-confident, more comfortable with yourself and more tuned into others and their needs.

Body Language

You may already possess self-confidence yet are unable to express it in a way that lets others perceive you as a leader. Did you know that 55 percent of any messages are delivered through body language? You may feel very self-confident, but if you have picked up any negative body language habits, they will give the wrong impression to those around you.

What are these negative body language messages?

Eye Contact

Let's start with eye contact. In normal conversation, you glance at a person for about a second and then glance away so that the other person doesn't think you are staring at them. If you avoid eye contact, it will probably be interpreted as a sign of low self-esteem, weakness or guilty feelings.

Posture

Women tend to carry their heads lower than men, walk with shorter, more erratic steps and slump their shoulders inward. All of these characteristics are often seen as a "weak" posture. The most personally powerful posture is almost military — spine and head erect and straight, arms at sides, with a 12-inch stride in walking.

Facial Expression

Women also tend to smile more than men do. Although this indicates a warmth toward the other person, it may also indicate a desire to please or "be nice." In business, a relaxed facial expression (not a poker face) is most appropriate. Smile back only when the other person smiles at you.

Proxemics

This is essentially territoriality. In other words, the use of space to define our territory. Men tend to take more space at a boardroom table — they spread out their papers, push their coffee cups aside and spread their elbows and knees wide. Women are more likely to "shrink" in on themselves, keeping their elbows and knees in tightly, neatly putting their papers directly in front of their seat. In a group, men move into the circle comfortably. Women may hold back and stand just outside the circle.

Remember, women tend to use body language that communicates a second-class status or less power. Holding the head slightly downward to avoid a direct stare, avoiding direct eye contact, rounding shoulders, and more-than-necessary smiles and nods are a few patterns to avoid. Men and women read these body signals subconsciously, which leads to the discounting of even the most persuasive, credible verbal comments.

You can increase your personal power tenfold by modifying a few body-language patterns.

Voice Patterns

Did you know that your voice will convey about 38 percent of your communication message to others? Many people equate a strong, deep male voice with power and authority, but women have some characteristic voice patterns that sometimes distract from their credibility.

As a woman, you may not want to have a male-sounding voice, but you can improve the powerful quality of your voice by working to make your voice strong, firm, relaxed, self-confident, appropriately loud, forceful, low-pitched and well-modulated.

Many women retain the voice pitch and tone of a little girl throughout their lives. You can lower the pitch of your voice with a little practice. Record your voice on tape; listen to it carefully. Rerecord and drop the pitch of your voice, imagining how you would sound if you were a great leader. Notice the difference between the two recordings?

One of the things you can do to improve the quality of your voice is to tape your telephone conversations. On playing them back, watch for voice tones that are apologetic, whiney, prissy, meek, tentative, imploring, nagging or schoolmarmish.

Some women speak so softly that it's difficult for others to hear. Practice adding some volume to your voice until you can do it comfortably. Men tend to have a naturally louder volume than women, so when talking with men, bring your volume up to match theirs. Otherwise, you'll sound meek and passive.

Pay particular attention to the habit of swinging the tone *upward* at the end of spoken statements, making them sound like questions. "I think that's a good *idea* (?)." If you've developed this speech habit, become consciously aware of it and force your voice to move lower at the end of a sentence, thus sounding more forceful and assertive.

Language Patterns

Language accounts for approximately seven percent of your communication message. Although it's a small portion of the overall message, it shouldn't be ignored. Watch for these particular negative speech patterns:

1. Women tend to use adjectives that add little meaning to the statement.

    "I think that's a *very, very* good idea."

    "I'm *incredibly* upset with the program."

    To see the difference, say these sentences without the adjectives. Notice how they become instantly powerful statements.

2. Women also tack little questions onto the end of declarative sentences. These questions add uncertainty and discount the comments.

    "It's time to get down to work, *don't you think?*"

    "I'd like to start now, *OK?*"

    Again, try saying these sentences without the add-on questions. They become powerful.

3. There is also a tendency to use disclaimers before an opinion or strong statement. These disclaimers are usually separated from the statement with a "but," which verbally erases the power of the statement. They also invite a challenge.

    "*I'm not really an expert, but* I think Plan B would be best."

    "*I probably shouldn't say anything, but* I need to have the report today."

4. Some use a lot of modifying phrases such as "maybe," "sort of" and "a little."

    "I'm *a little bit* worried about Gerald."

    "It's *sort of* an idea that might work, *maybe*."

5. Some women remove their own credibility by using apologies with a statement.

    "*I'm really sorry to bother you*, but I wonder if you could check your report?"

By taping your conversations, you'll soon become aware of any of these speech habits that you may be using. Remember, each one of them will detract from your personal power and credibility.

Professional Image

Did you know that people make a decision about you in seven seconds? That's all the time it takes for them to look you up and down and decide how to respond to you. Your appearance plays a great deal of importance in that first seven seconds. It tells about your attitude, your competence and your role in the company.

People selected for higher-level positions tend to look and act as if they fit the role, even before they're promoted.

Many articles have been written on how to dress for business success. Some basic guidelines to follow are:

- Simple lines, classic styles

- Neutral colors (gray, navy, black, brown, beige, tan)

- Clothes and accessories that are as expensive as you can afford

- Natural fibers (wool, cotton, linen, silk)

- Minimal, simple jewelry

- Simple, neat, natural hairstyles

You can always add your own touches of individuality and color with blouses, scarves and other accessories. The main point is to avoid "costumes" that detract from your main purpose: acceptance as a credible professional.

Self-Management

In order to be a polished, credible professional, it's necessary for you to take stock of yourself: your body language, your voice tones and language patterns, as well as your general clothing image. Together, they create a professional image and personal assertiveness that go a long way toward your effectiveness as a manager.

Take stock of your professional image. Answer yes or no to the following questions.

Body Language:	Yes	No

1. Do you:
   - Stand tall, shoulders back and head up?
   - Always make eye contact when talking with others?
   - Avoid folding your arms across your chest during conversations?
   - Keep your head up and erect?
   - Walk firmly and with an easy stride?
   - Sit erect in your chair?
   - Avoid leaning on the table or on other support?
   - Take your full space at a meeting table?
   - Move into a group when you want to talk with them?
   - Do you keep your face neutral when first meeting someone?

2. Do you:
   - Wait until the other person looks at you before making eye contact?
   - Smile when meeting another person for the first time?
   - Nod to show your agreement?
   - Arrange your papers on the table so that they don't go outside your "space"?
   - Keep your elbows in and knees tightly crossed when sitting with the group?
   - Wait until invited before moving into a group?
   - Keep your eyes averted when making negative comments?
   - Fold your arms when you're not speaking?
   - Keep your hands in your pockets?
   - Doodle or play with your pencil when you're not speaking?

Reflections

	Yes	No

Voice Tone:
1. Do you:
   - Try to match the loudness of your voice to the others in the group?
   - Speak clearly and slowly, even when you're nervous?
   - End your sentences with a downward inflection?
   - Pitch your voice in the lower end of your range?
   - Avoid sounding apologetic?

2. Do you:
   - Know that others complain that they can't hear you?
   - Often rush your words when saying something negative?
   - Avoid sounding pushy by adding a small upward inflection on the end?
   - Ignore the volume of others in the conversation?
   - Sound much younger than you are, especially on the telephone?

Speech Patterns:
1. Do you:
   - Try to speak with an economy of words?
   - Eliminate any unnecessary words or modifiers?
   - Use short, to-the-point sentences?

2. Do you:
   - Add qualifiers to strong statements?
   - Use long, involved sentences that run on?
   - Give too much information?

Reflections

Reflections

	Yes	No

Dress:

1. Do you:
   - Dress differently for work than for home?
   - Have one expensive "good" suit for special occasions?
   - Upgrade your wardrobe regularly?
   - Try to look like the next level up in management?
   - Study the dress habits of upper-level management in your business?
   - Avoid wearing outfits to work that stand out in a crowd?
   - Check for loose buttons, drooping hems, holes or runs in pantyhose, spots or stains on clothing, scuffed shoes or wrinkles each time you choose an outfit for work?

2. Do you:
   - Look the same at work as you do at home?
   - Love to try out new hairstyles and clothing at work?
   - Just grab anything out of the closet and put it on?
   - Think there's no point in getting "good" clothes just for work?
   - Often find a loose button or torn seam after you get to work?
   - Ignore fashion and wear clothing from your early years on the job?
   - Ignore weight gain or loss and wear the same clothes as before?

How Did Your Image Measure Up?

In each section, all "yes" answers for a question 1 and all "no" answers for a question 2 indicate that you're doing fine in that area. Any "no" answers to a question 1 or "yes" answers to a question 2 indicate that you have a need to improve in that particular area.

Reflections

5 EMPOWERING OTHERS

The most important people skill that a leader can have is the ability to empower others. Until the moment that you move into a leadership position, the need to empower others does not enter into your consciousness. But, as a leader, you are responsible for bringing a group of people together, creating a common vision and, most importantly, convincing, persuading, motivating even coercing them to peak performance.

To empower means to enable, allow or permit. There are two aspects to organizational empowerment:

1. Building, developing and increasing power through cooperation, sharing and working together, and

2. Making a commitment to common goals, taking risks, and demonstrating initiative and creativity

Empowerment is to encourage others to participate actively in the decision-making process. It allows them to achieve recognition, involvement and a sense of worth in their jobs, thus improving job satisfaction and morale.

How do you do all of that with the people you lead?

1. Determine that you are responsible for your group.

2. Accept your right to be the leader of this group.

3. Trust your group.

Once you have the mindset of a leader, you are ready to empower your team. Your first task is to enable them. This means you will give them permission to be participative members of the team. You will create opportunities for them to express their thoughts, ideas and opinions. And you will encourage them to listen and give feedback to one another.

When Mamie was appointed the team leader of the sales department, she immediately called a team meeting. She set an agenda, sent out memos to all the members and opened the meeting promptly.

Mamie used this initial meeting as a way to tell the group what she expected from them as their leader. She handed out a list of assignments and responsibilities. She then set the next meeting and dismissed the group.

Mamie felt pretty good about the way she handled the meeting. No one had any questions, there were no long-winded discussions, and everything was settled with a minimum of time and hassle.

However, as the weeks went by, Mamie found that the productivity of her team was decreasing, deadlines weren't met, and there was a general air of disinterest in the goals of the team. She continued to call meetings, each time telling the group what was expected of them. She pointed out where they weren't meeting her expectations and reminded them that their annual reviews would be affected by the success or failure of their team.

Much to her dismay, the energy of the group seemed to diminish, and the morale of the department plummeted. She couldn't figure out what had gone wrong. Why did she have to hang over them, pushing them to meet their deadlines, continually following up and calling them? Why couldn't her team just get on with the job they needed to do?

The lack of response from Mamie's team members is a good indication that they didn't feel part of a team. In fact, they probably felt that Mamie regarded them as no more than robotic subordinates whose only job was to do what they were told to do, with no discussion or leeway.

Mamie was using an **autocratic** management style that stifled the empowerment of her team.

Positional vs. Personal Power

One of the reasons that team members are reluctant to open up and communicate is that they see the team leader in a power position.

The habit of allowing the person in power to make all the decisions is strongly ingrained in people who have worked in a traditional organizational hierarchy. When you act as if you have the authority and power to make demands on your team, members correspondingly will treat your demands just as they do when they have little or no input. They will give lip service but no enthusiasm or energy.

What kind of power should the leader of a team demonstrate? Personal power!

Personal power is not conferred on you by higher authorities but comes from your own skills, abilities and experiences. It's a long way from the old positional power role of telling people what to do.

Using your personal power rather than your positional power greatly enables the team to work toward its goals. Here are some practical suggestions for using personal power in your leadership role:

1. Encourage the group to work together on decision-making. Strive for consensus, in which each person has an opportunity to participate. Mamie could have asked for suggestions on the best time for the team meetings to be held.

2. Allow members of the group to have some say in assignments. Sometimes their assessments of their own abilities are more accurate than yours, and they will often share tasks and work

together if given the opportunity. When Mamie found that the team was not getting the tasks done, she could have given them the opportunity to reassign tasks and realign responsibilities more in keeping with what they were most skilled at doing.

3. Give the team the responsibility, as a unit, for reviewing and evaluating its progress on tasks. Mamie did all the reviewing and evaluating. She also set the goals and determined the outcomes. This can be viewed as a group decision-making opportunity.

If you've ever been in a situation where you had no power or responsibility, you'll remember how you felt. In a meeting with no agenda, with orders from "on high," and with no discussion and no feedback, you probably felt frustrated, angry, apathetic, uninvolved. In a word — unempowered!

The best way to ensure enthusiasm, involvement and energy in your group is to let them take some of the responsibility. This is where the trust factor comes in. You must also trust them to take that responsibility seriously.

How do you encourage shared responsibility?

1. Set up assignments that require input and cooperation of several members.

2. Share all information.

3. Show members how their tasks are part of the big picture of your organization.

4. Encourage members to cross-train with each other, sharing skills and experience.

Empowered Communication

Empowering others means to encourage up, down and sideways communication. That is, to communicate up to management, down to subordinates and sideways to co-workers.

Using empowered communication with others means that you ask for feedback from your group. You listen carefully to the feedback, both positive and negative, and encourage an open discussion.

You don't feel threatened if someone in your group has a better idea than you. You don't stifle creative ideas just because they haven't been tried before. You don't squash someone else's enthusiasm.

In short, you see yourself as a facilitator, someone whose job it is to open up the lines of communication within the group.

Are you ready to empower others? Rate yourself on a scale of 1-5, with 1 being "not at all," and 5 being "always."

_____ 1. I feel anxious when members of my group don't treat me with the respect that I feel my position deserves.

_____ 2. I know that I can trust my subordinates to work hard and take responsibility.

_____ 3. I dislike spending the time it requires for everyone to give their opinions so that we can reach some kind of consensus.

_____ 4. I try to share as much information as possible with my group, telling them everything that I know about the issue.

_____ 5. I avoid bringing up problems because I don't want to give a negative impression.

_____ 6. I make sure there's plenty of opportunity for discussion and questions in our meetings.

_____ 7. I assign all tasks and responsibilities without input from my subordinates.

_____ 8. I like to give people an opportunity to work together on tasks, so they can learn new skills from each other.

_____ 9. I ask for all suggestions in writing. That avoids a lot of wasted time on endless discussions of ideas that won't work.

_____ 10. I like to work with my group on our goals and evaluate our progress together.

Reflections

How did you do?

The even-numbered statements are empowering statements.

The odd-numbered statements are indicative of an autocratic management style.

If you're an empowering leader, you'll have scored 4s and 5s on the even-numbered statements and 1s and 2s on the odd-numbered statements.

If you tend to be more autocratic in the way you lead others, you'll have scored 4s and 5s on the odd-numbered statements and 1s and 2s on the even-numbered statements.

You can also determine how you balance your management style between empowering and autocratic.

Add up your scores for all the even-numbered statements: _____ (Empowering)

Add up your scores for all the odd-numbered statements: _____ (Autocratic)

Here are some questions to reflect upon:

1. Which score was higher and by how much? What does this tell you about your style?

2. Based upon your scores, what can you do to be more empowering to your group? What do you want to start doing? Stop doing?

Reflections

6 MOTIVATING OTHERS

It's hard to know which comes first: motivation or empowerment. If empowerment is enabling people, then motivation is getting them going!

Many old-time managers will say that the paycheck is all the motivation that people need. If that isn't enough, lay it on the line. Tell them what is expected of them. Be direct. Be firm and use your authority. If that doesn't work, put them on notice. It's not the boss's job to spend a lot of time listening, fact-gathering, counseling, supporting or discussing alternatives.

However, today's leaders understand that, in the final analysis, motivation comes from *within* the person. A leader can't really motivate anyone; what she can do is take specific actions that encourage the inner motivation to perform well.

Tangible vs. Intangible Motivators

What are the motivators that a leader can use? There are two kinds:

1. General or tangible motivators

2. Personal or intangible motivators

The tangible motivators are such things as:

- Year-end bonus

- Good pension plan

- Parking privileges

- Company cafeteria

- Opportunity to buy company stock

- Training at company expense

- Travel allowance

- Comprehensive medical/dental plan

- Cost-of-living pay adjustments

- Annual leave plan recognizing length of service

- Comfortable, modern offices

- Recreation sponsored by the company

- Piped-in music

- Company-sponsored events, such as annual picnic, Christmas party, etc.

- Field trips

Some managers believe that these tangible motivators are all that count. If that is true, how come there are so many disenchanted employees who live for the weekend, put in marginal job performance, have no commitment to quality, have no loyalty for the company and don't like their jobs? One survey showed this very clearly:

- Only 23 percent of the workers said they were performing to full capacity.

- Nearly half (44 percent) said they gave just enough effort to get by on their jobs.

- Sixty-two percent of managers, workers and union officials believed people weren't working as hard as they used to.

- Fifty percent of the surveyed managers said there was no relationship between a job well-done and the paycheck.

There's a lot more to motivation than the tangible rewards in the workplace. Consider these intangible motivators:

- Job challenge

- Growth on the job

- Pleasant, cooperative associates

- Capable supervisors

- Recognition and praise for a job well-done

- Full delegation

- An understanding boss

- Clear-cut goals

- Effective responsibility

- Job security

- Involvement in decision-making

- Advancement opportunities

- Skill development

Monica works in a small printing shop. It's in the basement of an older downtown building in a poor part of town. The big room is crammed with printing equipment. There are no walls between areas, and the sound of the machines fills the air so that workers must shout back and forth to each other. The lunchroom is a counter with a coffeepot. The toilet facilities are communal.

Monica was hired as a receptionist, but when the boss (one of two brothers who started the business on a shoestring) found out she liked to draw, he put her on the pasteup desk. He quickly showed Monica the ropes and let her loose. One day, when one of the staff was off sick, Monica found herself helping at the collating machines.

When a big job comes in, everyone works until it's done. Sometimes, they're eating take-out pizza at midnight as the last sheet rolls off the old Heidelberg press.

There are no set lunch hours or coffee breaks. Everyone grabs time when they can. If Monica wants to go shopping on her lunch hour, it's not a problem if she's away longer than usual. She'll make up for it later.

Her paycheck isn't great. However, when a big job is finished, everyone gets a bonus. And, she can always make a little extra on overtime.

Why does Monica stay? Because she loves her job. She loves learning new skills, she enjoys her co-workers, and she sees real possibilities for advancement when the business takes off. She knows that the owners are thinking about a chain of printing shops in the future, and she's in the right place to benefit from expansion.

Best of all, Monica appreciates the praise that her boss gives her — he lets her know when she's done a good job. And, he's equally honest if Monica needs some coaching to bring her up to his standards.

When a worker's job is in a poorly lit, crowded office, with low pay, long working hours, no benefits and a no-frills environment, why would that worker give 100 percent to the job? And yet it happens. Almost all of us can remember working in such an environment and loving our jobs. We gave our time, effort and energy because we were *motivated* to do so, not by those tangible factors but by intangible motivators that triggered our desire to excel.

Recognizing the Manager's Role as Motivator

Effective managers are able to show their workers how meeting their job objectives will satisfy their needs and help them obtain some of the rewards they want most. The manager's behavior will have a motivating effect on workers to the extent that a worker's performance is rewarded and supported by the manager.

What kind of needs do workers have? In general, they can be classified into six categories:

1. **Achievement:** A chance to engage in independent problem-solving, to complete tasks and to see final results.

2. **Recognition:** Acknowledgment of accomplishment.

3. **The work itself:** Job content providing challenge, interest and variety as opposed to dull, boring activities.

4. **Responsibility:** Having full responsibility and accountability for results, including freedom to act, control and decide.

5. **Advancement:** Movement to a higher-level task or activity.

6. **Growth:** Learning, growing and expanding on the job.

Looking at this list, you can see how Monica's job in the printing shop met these needs and why she was *motivated* to do her best.

However, it's important for the manager to determine which needs will motivate which worker. Not everyone is motivated by the same things. Of all the actions you can take, the one that will have the most dramatic effect on the motivation environment of your group is matching the right person to the right job. You can get the right match by hiring people who fit the job and the group by transferring people within the group to achieve a better fit and by reorganizing jobs for a better fit.

Recognizing Socially Acquired Motivators

Psychologist David McClelland has developed an approach to motivation that says our needs are socially acquired from our culture and will vary from culture to culture.

> Helen, Betty and Kris are three friends who work together in the same company. They usually have lunch together and often go shopping after work. They all started with the company at the same time in the accounting department. Now, the position of supervisor has become open, and the three of them are eligible for the promotion. When they discuss their chances for promotion, they have differing viewpoints on what it will mean to them.

> Helen is concerned how a promotion will affect her time available for her family. She's also concerned what her co-workers will think if she's promoted over them. She hopes it won't cause any conflict or affect her friendly relationships in the department.

> Betty wants to be promoted. She has a lot of ideas she wants to bring into the department, and she's determined to push them through once she is in a position of power. She knows she can handle any problems that might result from her changes.

> Kris thinks her track record will speak for itself. She's proud of the new system she set up for accounts payable. It was her project from start to finish, and she's glad that she put all that extra time and effort into seeing its completion. She's sure it will make a difference in her promotability.

The three women have different motives that drive them:

- Helen has high affiliation needs. Her primary concern is people and relationships.

- Betty has high power needs. Her primary concern is how to get and use power.

- Kris has high achievement needs. Her primary concern is problem-solving and achieving modest goals.

You can see how differently each woman will behave if she is appointed supervisor.

As a manager, you will need to recognize these different socially acquired needs in your group. To motivate a worker, you must find work that will meet her need.

If you have a worker with affiliation needs, put her in a position of coordinator or integrator. She will also make a good teacher, coach and mentor and will want to directly help others. Give her a job that allows her to interact with numerous people on a daily basis.

Workers with strong power needs are usually upwardly mobile. You'll need to recognize that someone with this need is probably looking for opportunities to advance and move forward. Give her a job where she can personally direct co-workers. She'll appreciate being able to deal directly with the boss and to be reasonably free to come and go without a lot of direct supervision.

People who have achievement needs excel in positions where they can use their problem-solving skills. They're also good where commission work is involved or where they can see the results of their achievements. They'll want to know how well they are doing and will appreciate the freedom to set their own work pace.

How can you tell what your workers' needs are? Pay special attention to them and try to tune into what motivates them. What kinds of work give them the most satisfaction? How do they talk about their work? Which tasks do they do best? When have they excelled? When have they done less-than-adequate work?

Providing a Motivating Work Environment

In the movie "Nine to Five," the issue of a motivating work environment is addressed through comedy. The opening scenes of the company's office show desks in rows, "no talking" signs, blank walls, rules posted prominently and a "big brother is watching you" atmosphere.

Have you ever walked into an office like that and felt a chill in the air? People aren't talking to each other, there is no eye contact, the boss sits behind a closed door. The offices are sterile with no posters, no reflections of the people who work there.

In the movie, the workers revolt and change their working environment. In real life, it's not so easy.

Every organization has a distinctive climate or atmosphere. It is not something that has been stated in any manual or policy statement, but it's there. It takes many forms, from highly encouraging to highly discouraging.

A negative climate results when employees are subject to management behaviors they perceive as controlling, fear-inducing, punishing, shaming, blaming and judging. A positive climate results when managerial responses are involving, informing, rewarding, encouraging, supporting, trusting, sharing, caring, listening and growth-inducing.

In a negative climate, people become defensive and fearful, which in turn triggers the fight/flight/freeze response. They become angry, withdrawn or apathetic. They're resentful, evasive or passive. They may be openly antagonistic, they may have high absenteeism, or they may procrastinate or waste time.

> Grace's group has the highest production record in the company. Visitors from other departments are always surprised to find that there's a lot of laughter and talking going on within the group. They look like they're not working very hard, yet a lot of work is getting done.

Grace has high standards, but she works individually with each person in the group to help them achieve those standards. She gives a lot of feedback, both positive and negative, and is open to suggestions from the group. In fact, her door is always open, and her workers know that she can be approached for assistance when needed.

Grace gives her workers opportunities to use their creativity and determine new ways of doing the work. She often sets up "lunch and learn" meetings with special training videos, discussions and demonstrations.

A large chart on the wall shows how the production of the department ties in with the production of the rest of the company. A suggestion box sits prominently on a side table. Motivational posters, group photos and funny banners decorate the walls.

Each worker has her own particular area and is encouraged to make it personal with family photos, ornaments and posters.

What is Grace doing right? She's giving her people a motivational climate by providing:

1. **Meaning:** Work that has meaning has high standards, integrity and concern for customers.

2. **Contribution:** Opportunities to express creativity and initiative.

3. **Community:** People need to feel connected to one another and to believe that their work is worthwhile.

4. **Growth:** People experience movement, progress, interest and challenge.

5. **Influence:** Everyone has a say about decisions that may affect them.

The Final Analysis

You can't motivate anyone but yourself. Manipulation, occasional "rewards" and a pat on the back now and then do not motivate others. The key to motivation is to: a) determine what needs a worker has and b) determine what rewards a worker values. You can then structure job content and the work environment to enhance the worker's self-motivation.

What Motivates You?

Check the following motivators that have a force or influence on you and how you do your work. Then, rank the five checked items that have the most motivational significance for you.

____ Good working conditions	____Continuing growth on the job
____ Friendly associates	____ Recognition by peers
____ Full delegation	____ The paycheck
____ An understanding boss	____ Clear-cut goals
____ Pension plan	____ A job well-done
____ Well-furnished office	____ More responsibility
____ New, challenging assignments	____ Job security
____ Periodic pay increases	____ Special assignments
____ Hospital and medical plan	____ Vacation policy
____ Recognition by the boss	____ Annual bonus
____ Involvement in decision-making	____ Field trips
____ Advancement	____ Training courses

What did you find out about the kind of motivators that move you? Were they predominantly tangible or intangible?

Reflections

What Are Your Primary Socially Acquired Motivators?

For each of the following behaviors, indicate whether you received a reward for that behavior. Use R for rewarded behavior, A for anxiety-resulting and N for neutral behavior.

1. Taking over a situation _____
2. Sticking to your point of view _____
3. Being in control of others _____
4. Convincing others to do what you want them to do _____
5. Breaking a rule to reach a goal _____
6. Figuring out how to fix something _____
7. Taking "hard subjects" as electives _____
8. Getting good grades _____
9. Finishing a tough project _____
10. Competing with others _____
11. Following instructions _____
12. Pleasing others _____
13. Patching up a quarrel _____
14. Helping someone else _____
15. Participating in a group _____

Generally speaking, the items marked with R will indicate the behaviors that form part of your motivating needs.

- Questions 1-5 reflect power-oriented behavior.
- Questions 5-10 reflect achievement-oriented behavior.
- Questions 11-15 reflect affiliation-oriented behavior.

Which group had the most R's?

Reflections

What Motivates Others?

Write down the name of someone you work with (or who works for you). Based on your observation of how this person works, conversations you've had and what you've heard, what do you think this person's motivators are?

a) Tangible motivators:

b) Intangible motivators:

c) Socially acquired motivators:

What kind of job would be best for this person to do?

What can you do to motivate this person to do an excellent job?

Reflections

7 RESOLVING CONFLICT

The "Being Liked" Dilemma

Everyone wants to be liked. Being liked is great for the ego — it can help you establish a strong, personal power base. However, many women managers tend to be unaware that their primary motive is to be liked.

If you remember the discussion on socially acquired motivators from the previous chapter, you'll probably agree that most women have received the greatest rewards and reduced more anxieties through affiliation-oriented behavior rather than through power- and achievement-oriented behaviors. "Being nice," "pleasing others" and "obeying the rules" are primary directives for many young women, even today.

Unfortunately, these behaviors erode credibility. If you show any reluctance to confront poor performance, to delegate a messy task or to show your authority, you'll become ineffective.

Don't trade being respected for being liked. There's no need to trade off. You can be both, but you must be respected above all else.

When you must deal with a conflict with another person, deal with it directly, using your authority and power to settle the matter.

Conflict: Positive or Negative?

What is your attitude toward conflict? Is it positive or negative? If your answer is negative, then you need to re-examine the process, purpose and end results of conflict. The leader's attitude toward conflict determines whether conflict occurs openly and whether it is a positive or negative force.

Perhaps the most common way to view conflict is to see it as something undesirable, something that should be avoided at all costs. If conflict is poorly handled or ignored, it does create problems:

- Decreased productivity

- Erosion of trust

- Formation of coalitions — polarized positions

- Secrecy

- Morale problems

- Wasted time

- Paralyzed decision-making

However, if conflict is handled properly, it can provide numerous benefits to both the individuals involved and their organizations:

- Increased motivation

- Enhanced problem- and solution-identification

- Group cohesiveness

- Reality adjustment

- Increased knowledge/skill

- Enhanced creativity

- Contribution to goal attainment

- Incentive for growth

Your Conflict-Management Style

How do you handle conflict? There are five universally accepted approaches to conflict management. No one approach will work in all situations. It's important for you to develop the ability to use each style in the appropriate situation.

Penny is the supervisor of a large word processing group for her company. Fifty-two clerks report directly to her. They are a diverse group: different ethnic backgrounds, colors, male and female, young and old. Sometimes, Penny feels like a firefighter, putting out one blaze after another. One week, the problems are all about a new scheduling system.

On Monday, Penny sits down with three of her staff who are having a problem with scheduling issues. She listens to all sides, asks for their input, makes suggestions and helps them reach a consensus. It takes most of the morning to do this.

On Tuesday, Penny is behind on some of her own work, so when Bill and Mary come to her with their scheduling problem, she works out a compromise with them. This way, she saves some time.

On Wednesday, Penny tells Amanda that her work schedule cannot be adjusted and that she's to do her work and stop complaining.

On Thursday, still feeling guilty about her summary treatment of Amanda, Penny gives in and allows Corrine to make her own scheduling changes.

By Friday of a rough week, Penny just goes into her office and puts out the "do not disturb" sign. She makes it clear she doesn't want to deal with any more issues. The clerks can work them out for themselves.

Penny's staff complain among themselves that Penny is hard to read, often arbitrary and often unfair in her treatment of them. They never know how she's going to react, and, as a result, they never feel that issues are resolved to their satisfaction.

Penny doesn't know how else she can handle the conflicts that keep arising. "I've tried everything," she tells her boss. "Nothing seems to work with them."

What are the five styles of conflict?

1. Collaborating Style

2. Compromising Style

3. Dominating Style

4. Placating Style

5. Avoiding Style

These styles are determined by two sets of factors: relationships/feelings and control/authority.

The following diagram illustrates how the styles are determined.

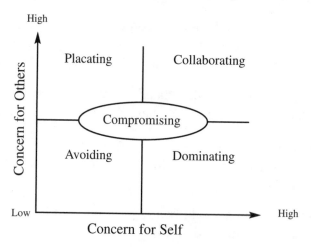

1. When there is a high regard for relationships and a high need to retain some control or authority, the collaborating style is used. Penny used this style on Monday.

2. When relationships and authority issues aren't so important, compromise is used. Penny compromised on Tuesday.

3. When relationships or feelings aren't considered and authority/control is available, the dominating style is used. Penny dominated Amanda on Wednesday.

4. When relationships or feelings are primary and authority/power is sacrificed, placating is used. Penny placated on Thursday because she felt (feelings) guilty.

5. When neither relationships nor authority issues play a part, the avoidance style is used. On Friday, Penny didn't care how her employees felt and didn't want to make the effort to exert her authority. She used avoidance to deal with the conflict.

Penny's problems weren't caused by her use of the conflict styles but her inappropriate use of the styles. She needs to determine what style is most appropriate for each situation.

When to Use Each Style

1. The **Collaborating Style** is behavior that is strongly cooperative and assertive. It reflects a "win-win" approach. Both parties win. This style represents a desire to maximize joint outcomes. This style is best used when:

    •   There is time available to work toward a mutual outcome.

    •   There is mutual trust among the parties.

    •   There is a sharing of power.

    •   There is a mutual desire to preserve the relationship.

    •   Feelings are considered.

2. The **Compromising Style** is behavior that is between cooperative and assertive. It's a give-and-take process and can involve negotiation and a series of concessions. However, because of the concessions made, both parties may feel that they have lost a little in the process. It is best used when:

   • A decision must be reached quickly.

   • Each party has something to give up.

   • Each party recognizes that there may be a loss of relationship and trust.

3. The **Dominating Style** is assertive but uncooperative. It reflects a "win-lose" approach in that only one person or group wins. It usually results in an eroding of the relationship and may involve an abuse of power. It should only be used when:

   • An emergency involving quick action is the issue.

   • There is no discussion or room for compromise.

   • The orders are from "above" and must be implemented.

   • There is no relationship to preserve.

4. The **Placating Style** involves behavior that is unassertive yet cooperative. In this style, one party will "give in" for the common good. It is considered a "lose-win" style since the issue is not resolved to everyone's satisfaction. It can be used when:

   • The issue isn't important enough to be involved in.

   • The most important thing is to preserve the relationship.

   • Feelings are very much in the forefront and must be considered.

   • You have no power in the situation.

5. The **Avoiding Style** involves both unassertive and uncooperative behavior. It is a "lose-lose" style. We use this style to stay out of conflicts or remain neutral. This approach is a decision to let the conflict work itself out. It can be used when:

    •   Time is needed for emotions to cool off.

    •   The issue isn't directly related to you.

    •   You have no power in the situation.

Do you know your conflict style? Take this quiz and find out. For each of the statements, rank the five answers from 1-5:

5 — This is most like me.   2 — This is sometimes like me.
4 — This is usually like me.   1 — This is not at all like me.
3 — This is somewhat like me.

This means that you are assigning priority numbers to the five answers, with the number 5 indicating which statement is most like you down to 1 indicating which statement is least like you.

1. When you have strong feelings in a conflict situation, do you:

_____ A. Enjoy the emotional release and sense of exhilaration and accomplishment?

_____ B. Enjoy the challenge of the conflict?

_____ C. Become serious and concerned about how others are feeling and thinking?

_____ D. Find it frightening because someone will get hurt — emotionally or physically?

_____ E. Become convinced there is nothing you can do to resolve the issue?

2. What's the best result you can expect from a conflict?

_____ A. Conflict helps people face facts.

_____ B. Conflict cancels out extremes in thinking so a strong middle ground can be reached.

_____ C. Conflict clears the air, enhances commitment and results.

_____ D. Conflict demonstrates the absurdity of self-centeredness and draws people closer together.

_____ E. Conflict lessens complacency and assigns blame where it belongs.

3. When you have authority in a conflict situation, do you:

_____ A. Put it straight and let others know your view?

_____ B. Try to negotiate the best settlement?

_____ C. Ask for other viewpoints and suggest that a position be found that both sides might try?

_____ D. Go along with the others, providing support where you can?

_____ E. Keep the encounter impersonal, citing rules if they apply?

Reflections

4. When someone takes an unreasonable position, do you:

_____ A. Lay it on the line and say that you don't like it?

_____ B. Let him know in casual, subtle ways that you're not pleased, by possibly distracting with humor and avoiding direct confrontation?

_____ C. Call attention to the conflict and explore mutually acceptable solutions?

_____ D. Keep your misgivings to yourself?

_____ E. Let your actions speak for you, possibly using withdrawal or lack of interest?

5. When you become angry with a peer, do you:

_____ A. Explode without giving it much thought?

_____ B. Smooth things over with a good story?

_____ C. Express your anger and invite a response?

_____ D. Compensate for your anger by acting the opposite of your feelings?

_____ E. Remove yourself from the situation?

6. When you find yourself disagreeing with other members about a project, do you:

_____ A. Stand by your convictions and defend your position?

_____ B. Appeal to the logic of the group in the hope of convincing at least a majority that you are right?

_____ C. Explore points of agreement and disagreement, then search for alternatives that take everyone's views into account?

_____ D. Go along with the group?

_____ E. Not participate in the discussion or feel bound by any decision made?

7. When one group member takes a position in opposition to the rest of the group, do you:

_____ A. Point out publicly that the dissenting member is blocking the group and suggest that the group move on without him or her if necessary?

_____ B. Make sure the dissenting member has a chance to communicate her objections so that a compromise can be reached?

_____ C. Try to uncover why the dissenting member views the issue differently so that the group's members can re-evaluate their own positions?

_____ D. Encourage members to set the conflict aside and go on to more agreeable items on the agenda?

_____ E. Remain silent because it is best to avoid becoming involved?

Reflections

8. When you see conflict emerging in your team, do you:

_____ A. Push for a quick decision to ensure that the task is completed?

_____ B. Avoid outright confrontation by moving the discussion toward a middle ground?

_____ C. Share with the group your impression of what is going on so that the nature of the impending conflict can be discussed?

_____ D. Relieve the tension with humor?

_____ E. Stay out of the conflict as long as it is of no concern to you?

9. In handling conflict among group members, do you:

_____ A. Anticipate areas of resistance and prepare responses to objections prior to open conflict?

_____ B. Encourage your members to be prepared by identifying in advance areas of possible compromise?

_____ C. Recognize that conflict is healthy and press for the identification of shared concerns and/or goals?

_____ D. Promote harmony on the grounds that the only real result of conflict is the destruction of friendly relations?

_____ E. Submit the issue to an impartial arbitrator?

10. In your view, what might be the reason for the failure of one group to work with another?

_____ A. Lack of a clearly stated position or failure to back up the group's position.

_____ B. Tendency of groups to force their leaders to abide by the group's decision, as opposed to promoting flexibility, which would facilitate compromise.

_____ C. Tendency of groups to enter negotiations with a win-lose perspective.

_____ D. Lack of motivation on the part of the group's members to live peacefully with the other group.

_____ E. Irresponsible behavior on the part of the group's leaders, resulting in the leaders placing emphasis on maintaining their own power positions rather than addressing the issues involved.

Reflections

Your Score

Add up your assigned scores for each letter and enter them below.

A _____ DOMINATING STYLE

B _____ COMPROMISING STYLE

C _____ COLLABORATING STYLE

D _____ PLACATING STYLE

E _____ AVOIDING STYLE

Your highest score indicates your predominant conflict-management style. This is the style you use when you feel confident, powerful, and in control of the situation.

However, your next-highest score indicates your conflict-management style when you are stressed, emotional, or feeling powerless, angry or weak.

Reflections

8 DEALING WITH SEXUAL HARASSMENT AND SEXISM

Sexual Harassment

Sexual harassment is an unwanted behavior that interferes with the ability to work in an atmosphere free of intimidation. In its more severe form, it creates an implicit or explicit condition for employment and promotion. It's an ugly game that can be a subtle or coercive pressure for sexual activity. It's demeaning and frightening to the woman (or man) involved.

Two Truths About Sexual Harassment

1. Sexual harassment is pervasive in the workplace. A poll conducted by the National Association of Female Executives found that 53 percent of its 1,300 members have been victims of sexual harassment.

2. Men and women view sexual harassment differently. Men are more likely to rationalize the behavior with such comments as "She asked for it" and "It was just a flirtation — she took it too seriously."

   Jackie is the secretary of the Sales Department. Nine of the 12 sales reps are male, and Jackie enjoys the give-and-take of the daily workplace chatter. She always tells people that she's not a prude, and she can laugh at a joke as readily as the next person. She's not too shy to tell a couple of jokes of her own, either. However, lately Greg has been telling some very sexually explicit jokes, and he sent her a pornographic picture via e-mail. Jackie isn't sure what to do.

She doesn't want to spoil the easygoing camaraderie in the department. She's not even sure if Greg realizes how inappropriate his behavior is. In fact, she wonders if she may have brought it on herself by entering into the spirit of office joke-telling. Finally, she goes to Greg and tells him she doesn't like his jokes or pictures.

Greg acts surprised by her reaction. "I was only kidding," he tells her.

"Well, please don't do it again," Jackie counters.

The next day, another pornographic picture arrives on Jackie's desk.

When does the office sex game become sexual harassment? When the behavior is unwanted, unsolicited and nonreciprocal. The latest legislation now includes "the creation of a hostile environment" as grounds for sexual harassment. This is as much an issue for men as it is for women.

Can Jackie claim that she was sexually harassed? What do you think?

As a leader and manager, you may need to know more about what individuals and organizations can do to avoid harassment problems, what you should tell a harassed employee to do, and how you should resolve complaints and conflicts. Again, your male employees are as great a concern as your female employees.

Today we can't afford to allow any man or woman to persist in actions that constitute sexual harassment. To do so would signal to others that such behavior may be condoned by you and would set a poor example for the entire work team.

What do you do if a member of your work team comes to you and complains that he or she has been harassed? First of all, be aware that you have a responsibility to respond to his or her complaint. By law, you must investigate all complaints.

1. Take sexual harassment complaints as seriously as other conflicts and investigate them as thoroughly.

2. Keep such matters entirely confidential.

3. Find out what the complainant wants and try to accommodate that person.

4. Carefully investigate. Look for documentation, witnesses, confidants, observers.

5. Use disciplinary procedures set out by your organization.

6. Make sure no one retaliates against the complainant, no matter what the outcome.

What if *you* are the victim of sexual harassment? What if the harassing behavior escalates? How do you deal with it, knowing that confrontation and/or conflict will be present?

A Seven-Step Strategy for Dealing With Harassment

1. Talk privately to the person committing the harassment. State that you're not interested and want the harassment to stop; confront early.

2. Tell others what is happening and elicit their support.

3. Keep a detailed log of what is said, when, where, and under what circumstances.

4. Write a letter to be placed in your personnel file.

5. Contact your supervisor, or, if the person harassing you is your supervisor, go up one level and explain what is going on. Go to your human resources department. Indicate that you've documented the harassment and have spoken to others. If you have witnesses, say so then.

6. If no action is taken, lodge a formal complaint with the Equal Employment Opportunity Commission (EEOC).

7. Consider consulting an attorney who specializes in such cases.

Sexism

Sometimes, it's not overt sexual harassment that is the problem but sexism. Prejudice based on gender is a form of inequality that begins at home. Myths and stereotypes about masculine and feminine roles are rampant and misleading. Women in Western culture have traditionally been viewed as a wholly different species from men, invariably an inferior species.

Most career women must overcome internal barriers (discussed in chapter one) and external barriers to workplace success that are rooted in the North American culture. External barriers include the glass ceiling, inflexible work arrangements and pay disparity.

What happens when a woman becomes a manager over men? A recent survey of men showed some typical stereotypes of women in management:

- Women obsess over getting one small thing right, and it's blown out of proportion.

- Some women are detail-oriented, not conceptual — no sense of corporate mission or the big picture.

- Women are too sensitive, taking things too personally.

- Some women don't get down to business fast enough. First you have to spend time with them on a personal level.

- Women are harder on other women. There's more pettiness and jealousy.

- When two women are at each other's throats, it ruins the spirit of the whole team.

- When women bond together against men, it's demoralizing.

- Unmarried women bosses make men nervous, especially if their work is their life. They can work 14-hour days because they have no home life.

- Women don't conceal anger or bitterness as well as men.

- Men would rather work for men. Getting a performance review from a woman is a bit like getting lectured by one's mother.

Men and women working together inevitably brings a degree of frustration and conflict into the workplace. How can a woman live all her life cast as an inferior simply because of her gender? Frustration is building in men as they see their male privilege slipping away from them.

There are indeed overtly biased men and women in the workplace. Unless they have extreme power to make or break your career, ignore them. It's no longer socially acceptable to be outwardly and verbally biased. It's the covert bias that causes you the most trouble. Generally, most biased comments, behaviors and attitudes are not known by the sender. In fact, when you confront them, they are surprised that you're offended.

> Gwen is the team leader for a group of all-male technicians. She's found it hard to make the transition from one of the group to team leader. She feels that her group members don't take her seriously, don't listen to her, treat her differently from other male team leaders they've had, and disparage all her attempts to set goals and get things done. She tells her friends that they're all "sexist."

Gwen is not alone in her situation. Many women have to deal with conflicts arising from managing men. Here are four typical scenarios of sexism and how to deal with them:

1. Men may not know how to treat you. They're not sure whether they should open the door for you, lift a heavy box for you or offer to drive the car. In other words, they're having difficulty separating your female role from your professional role. Consequently, you'll need to take the initiative. In short, you'll need to establish your credibility. Make it clear you want to be treated as they would treat any other manager, and if you need help, you'll ask for it. "Could you carry that box for me? Thanks." (Note: Don't go into explanations of weakness. "That box is so heavy, and I'm just a

woman. Do you think you could use those big muscles and carry it for me? Oh, you're so kind. Thank you, thank you.")

2. Male subordinates may be concerned whether you can play the political game or use the informal network system. This is because they don't know if you have the power to help them if they need it. We'll talk more about learning the political ropes of your organization in a later chapter of this book, but for now, be aware that you'll need to do your homework thoroughly. You need to know who has power in your organization, how to influence that power, and how to use your own power to get what you want. Don't be afraid to drop names, either. References to lunch with Ms. Top Dog or a conversation with Ms. Division Head help calm their concerns.

3. Men may treat you like a mother figure. Your success as a manager requires that you steer around other people's stereotypes about the ways women behave and the roles women can have. Be wary of being cast as a "mother figure" by the men in your group. If you find yourself dispensing advice, cookies and aspirin, stop immediately! And never, under any circumstances, offer to sew on a button, make the coffee or organize a party. That's a mom's job.

4. Men may treat you with disrespect or a condescending attitude. Confront this behavior immediately — the longer you let it go, the worse it becomes. One of the best methods to use is the five-step approach:

    — *When you ...*

    — *I feel ...*

    — *Because ...*

    — *I want ...*

    — *Do you agree/understand?*

Since women focus on making personal connections, establishing rapport, cooperating with others and playing down their expertise, you must help men understand that these behaviors do not necessarily denote weakness, lack of confidence or incompetence.

What Is Your "Take" on Sexual Harassment?

1. Which of these statements comes closest to your overall view of sexual harassment?

    A. I think it's a very real problem, and I'm willing to get involved to solve it.

    B. I don't think about it too much — it's never been a problem for me.

    C. I think that too much has been made of it, and it's become the latest "workplace issue."

    D. I think it still may be a problem in some areas, but in today's modern high-tech society, there's no room for it in our fast-paced, aggressive businesses.

2. Which of these statements do you agree with:

    A. Sexual harassment is an issue all right, but I think issues like pay equity and equal promotional opportunity are a lot more important.

    B. I don't understand why a woman doesn't just say "no" when she thinks someone is harassing her.

    C. If the behavior is continuing, the woman didn't give a clear, unequivocal "no" to the harasser.

    D. A lot of women yell "sexual harassment" if a man just looks at them.

    E. It's pretty stuffy and prudish to get all uptight about a few jokes or pictures in the workplace. Look at the stuff we see on TV every day.

Reflections

3. In your opinion, which of these would constitute sexual harassment?

    A. A man puts his arm around your shoulders while looking at your project on the desk.

    B. Persistent requests for a date even though you've told him you're not interested.

    C. Telling dirty jokes in the lunchroom, especially if the person knows that your face turns red, and you get embarrassed.

    D. Personal remarks about your breasts or legs.

    E. A hint from your supervisor that you could have time off if you went to lunch with him.

4. What would you tell her to do if a close friend or relative confided to you that she was being harassed by her boss, the owner of the business?

    A. Quit the job.

    B. Threaten to tell his wife, girlfriend or others.

    C. Tell the harasser that the behavior is inappropriate and must be stopped.

    D. File a complaint right away.

    E. Get a good lawyer.

    F. Find out if others have been harassed by him and file a class action.

    G. Grin and bear it to protect her job.

Reflections

Answer Key

1. Statement A indicates that you're ready to take on any issues that might arise for you as a team leader, manager or supervisor. The other statements indicate a lack of understanding or preparedness on your part.

2. All of the statements are common misconceptions and myths about sexual harassment.

3. Each one of these could be a case for sexual harassment.

4. The correct course of action is statement C, followed by statement D.

Something for you to think about:

What do your answers tell you about how you might react if a member of your team came to you to deal with a sexual harassment complaint?

What are some areas where you have to adjust your thinking?

Reflections
Reflections

9 PERFORMANCE APPRAISALS AND DISCIPLINE

Performance Appraisals

Many managers look forward to the performance appraisal interview as much as they do to having root canal work done! Few see it as a valuable tool for building rapport with an employee and for creating successes in the department. Their responses to the performance appraisal runs from "I'll just rate the elements on the form on the high side, and it'll be over and done with in ten minutes" to "Bill gets so defensive when I try to tell him what went wrong" to "I don't know what to talk about — it's just another one of those time-wasters dreamed up by the human resources department."

Sometimes your own experiences with performance appraisals have caused you to see them as negative. Remember, performance appraisals are not a forum for criticism. This is too narrow a view. Criticism and feedback are only part of the process. Performance appraisals are important to the employee, the supervisor and the organization. Appraising performance is part of the control process that is so important in keeping the efforts of people on track, accomplishing goals and objectives. Using the following guidelines can make the performance-appraisal interview a worthwhile, highly productive experience.

1. **Preparation:** Be certain to prepare in advance for the session. Think in terms of:

    - What was accomplished and what was not
    - What you'd like to see done in the following time period
    - The major development needs of the employee

2. **Mindset:** You want this session to be a positive experience. Think of the forthcoming meeting as a joint planning session. Avoid dominating the session. Instead, focus on strengthening the relationship with your staffer, laying the groundwork for high accomplishment in the following time period, and planning for the next phase of work.

3. **Time allotments:** Don't treat the session like that trip to the dentist — to get in and out as quickly and painlessly as possible. Allot enough time for the meeting so that matters of mutual concern can be discussed thoroughly and meaningfully in a relaxed way. Be sure to turn off the phone and plan not to be interrupted.

4. **Communication patterns:** You'll want your staffer to do most of the talking because this is his opportunity to have you one-on-one. Use good listening skills and avoid any temptation to take over. Remember, you know your point of view — now find out his.

5. **Praise for performance:** Use the session to express your appreciation for work well-done. Everyone appreciates praise and recognition from the boss. Don't overlook opportunities to provide positive reinforcement to the extent possible.

6. **Discuss performance failures:** Avoid dwelling on past mistakes, blaming, faultfinding or petty criticisms. Regard poor performance areas as opportunities to create learning experiences. Don't fall into the trap of "appraisal by surprise" — that is, dredging up negative events that were never discussed previously with the employee. The inevitable reaction will be resentment and "Gee, if I'd known that was a problem, I would have done something about it. You should have told me when it happened."

7. **Closing the session:** You want to end the session on a high note. Make sure your staffer feels good about what he has accomplished and is eager to move on to new goals.

Dealing With Marginal Performers

> Marianne is dreading her performance appraisal with Celeste. "There's nothing good to tell her," says Marianne. "How can I give praise when all I have is a long list of behavior problems and performance failures?"
>
> Marianne knows that this is going to be a tough interview. If Celeste doesn't make some behavioral changes, she will be disciplined and perhaps even fired by Marianne. "I'm not sleeping at night, I'm so stressed-out about this," says Marianne. "Where do I start? What do I do? No one ever trained me for this kind of personnel stuff!"

Isn't that how you feel sometimes? No one trained you for the tough supervisory issues, yet so much depends on your doing it well — the morale of your staff, your credibility in the organization, the relationship between yourself and the employee.

Before your interview with a marginal performer, sit down and prepare yourself adequately for the meeting. Your first task is to analyze the problem employee's performance. Describe it in full. Actually write it down objectively and specifically. Use Who, What, Where, Why, When and How as headings for the description.

Then, identify the cost of this behavior. The cost can range from somewhat irritating to lower productivity to lowered team morale. The degree of cost will determine the severity of the negative behavior and of your reaction to it.

Gather documentation. What evidence do you have of this behavior? What testimony is there from others? Do you have any specific reports that you can use for reference?

Finally, look at your own performance. Did you fail with this employee in any way? Was there something you could have or should have done before the behavior reached this point? Is there anything you can do to turn this employee around?

When it comes time to confront the employee, remember these four guidelines:

1. Be descriptive, not judgmental.

2. Be supportive, not authoritative.

3. Reflect equality, not superiority.

4. Be accepting, not dogmatic.

Disciplining Employees

It's inevitable that you will be confronted with situations requiring disciplinary actions. Some of the more common situations are excessive absenteeism, tardiness, inadequate work performance and poor attitudes that interfere with the work of others. Most of us tend to put off dealing with the situation. However, if you do that, your other employees will begin to bend the rules to get away with similar violations.

Your workers want you to be assertive. They admire a sense of fairness that includes equal rights for all. Most of them will resent seeing a co-worker getting away with something.

When it's necessary to confront workers with poor results or unacceptable actions, use a problem-solving approach assertively. Focus on what can be done next, how to solve the problem, and how similar problems can be avoided in the future. Where possible, tie desirable behavior to achieving objectives a worker has set for his job.

Avoid the trap of comparing or implying comparison of one subordinate to another. Focus on the worker's own performance, according to the standards and objectives the two of you have agreed on previously. Remember, the purpose of disciplinary action is not to punish but to improve the employee's future behavior.

The following six rules, known as Douglas McGregor's "hot stove rules" relate to the disciplinary process:

1. **Discipline should be immediate.** The longer the delay, the less effective it is. Just as the touched hot stove gives immediate feedback, so should your discipline.

2. **Discipline should provide advance warning.** Prior warning, rather than unexpected discipline, is the best and fairest feedback tool. Just as a hot stove gives warning by color and heat, employees should be informed of the rules and the penalties for breaking them.

3. **Discipline should be marked by consistency.** Just as the hot stove burns everyone alike, so should you treat everyone alike when discipline is involved. Also, the hot stove burns everyone every time it is touched. This means not only applying the same penalties, but applying them consistently. There is no place for favoritism.

4. **Discipline must be on an impersonal basis.** You must focus on the behavior, not on the person. Remember that the hot stove punishes behavior alone, burning people for what they do, not for who they are.

5. **Use appropriate punishment only.** The old maxim of "the punishment fits the crime" still holds true. Light punishment for a heavy offense will be ignored. Again, the hot stove burns deeper with a longer touch than with a lighter one.

6. **Discipline with a regard to future relationships.** Treat the offender with grace, as a one-time errant person, not as a lifelong rules violator. The hot stove is a one-time pain, and most people learn a lesson from it. Don't hold grudges and do welcome the employee back onto the team. Your attitude is that it is a one-time mistake.

Termination of Employment

Suppose you have to fire someone. What do you do then? This is probably the worst nightmare of most supervisors and leaders. Basically, three requirements must be met before you terminate an employee:

1. The action taken should be based solely on performance, and every possible opportunity must have been provided for the employee to improve his work.

2. There has been full documentation of the worker's inability to meet clear-cut job requirements.

3. The personnel department has been contacted to ensure that the termination follows the organization's guidelines and that there won't be a case for wrongful dismissal.

Your anxiety about a termination session is both normal and healthy. It is a sign that you are a caring, feeling person involved in a difficult task. Help employees realize that termination is painful for everyone; you and the organization would like everyone to succeed, and you wish them well.

How well does your present performance-appraisal system meet goals?

Use the rating system 1-5.

> Scale: 5 — Always, 4 — Usually, 3 — Occasionally,
> 2 — Seldom, 1 — Never

1. Increases the employee's understanding of job role and the employer's expectations _____

2. Improves employee morale _____

3. Upholds professional standards _____

4. Increases employee's self-awareness of job performance _____

5. Maintains discipline _____

6. Rewards superior performance _____

7. Produces competition among employees _____

8. Reinforces boss/employee relationship _____

9. Improves employee's performance skills _____

10. Weeds out inferior employees _____

11. Increases employee's self-confidence and self-esteem _____

12. Informs supervisors/upper management of employee's performance _____

13. Provides basis for awards and/or promotions _____

14. Improves supervisor/employee relationship _____

15. Provides basis for changing financial compensation _____

Reflections

Scoring

Add up your total score.

- 60-70: You have an excellent performance-appraisal system in place.

- 30-60: There is room for improvement.

- 15-29: A trip to the dentist might be more useful than your performance appraisals!

Reflections

10 DEVELOPING YOUR TEAM

Building vs. Development

An effective team does not "just happen." It is the result of concerted efforts on the part of the team leader to both build and develop the team. These two activities are not mutually exclusive but do involve separate processes.

Building a Team

Used when:

- The team needs to get back on track.

- The team is experiencing decreased productivity.

- Conflict is present.

- Poor communication, apathy, no cooperation and low trust exist among team members.

- A merger or acquisition has occurred.

- A new team leader is appointed.

- A major reorganization or downsizing is implemented.

- New responsibilities are added to the team.

Developing a Team

Used as an ongoing process to:

- Upgrade team performance

- Improve staff meetings

- Improve problem-solving

- Develop feedback systems

- Develop conflict-management systems

Most typically, team-building will be carried out by an outside facilitator, frequently off-site. Team-development improvements are made by the team and its leader, utilizing their own skills and resources.

How Teams Function

A team-building/development function begins when group members recognize a problem in the way they function together, set goals, allocate work or relate to each other:

- Data is shared.

- Perceptions of issues/problems are discussed.

- Problem is analyzed.

- Underlying key issue is diagnosed.

- The group plans specific actions to resolve issue.

- The plan is evaluated.

    Jan is a new team leader. She inherited her team when its previous leader was promoted. She also inherited a lot of baggage with her team. One member was a best friend of the previous leader and was accustomed to being a favorite. One member believes that he should have been made team leader, not some outsider from another department. Another member is just returning after an extended sick leave for burnout and is still feeling rather fragile. Another member is much older than Jan and has been with the company a lot longer.

Jan's new team also has its own set of norms — the way it always does things. Meetings generally start 15-20 minutes late. Bill always speaks first. Maria is expected to take things personally and pout. Coffee and donuts are always ordered midmeeting. Cell phones are not turned off. Team members come and go as they please.

The team members have been together for nearly two years. They know each other well and often get together after work for social occasions. They have their own in-jokes.

The work assignments haven't been changed since the team was first formed. No real assessment has been done of individual strengths and weaknesses. There are no clear-cut goals. Jan isn't sure they even know why they are a team.

You may have an experience similar to Jan's. What do you do with a team to make it productive, dynamic and most of all, *yours*.

Stay Focused on the Task

Your job is to be a team leader, not to make friends. Keeping that in mind:

- Keep cool and make changes in a reasonable and an orderly way. Don't try to change everything all at once. Jan might begin with an on-time start to her meetings. This will signal that more changes will eventually follow.

- Do not try to placate or appease. Jan knows she has one or two team members who have a reason not to like her. She'll keep reminding herself that that is "their problem" not hers.

- Do not choose favorites. It's tempting to lean on that one team member who seems genuinely glad to have you as the team leader but don't fall into the trap of playing favorites. Jan's predecessor did that, and it only makes the team weaker.

- Let the team know that you are assessing the situation, that you are going to make changes as needed, and that you appreciate their knowledge, ability and cooperation.

Four Essential Team-Building Development Activities

1. Clarify employee roles

Your skill in team development is twofold:

1. To make the individual team members function well together

2. To discover the abilities of your team members

Before you make any sweeping changes in task assignments or team groupings, take the time to get to know the individual team members. Ask them what they like to do in their jobs. Look at their past performance history. Where did they excel? Where did they have problems?

2. Build trust

For teams, trust is one of the great enablers. The major "no trust" issues occur when people stop communicating, resulting in confusion, tension, reduction in productivity, conflict, frustration and inability to get the job done. How can this be prevented?

Unfortunately, you can't teach trust to your team members; you can only build it. Trust develops over time as team members experience one another in situations that call for it.

What can you do as a team leader?

- Behave consistently in responding to others.

- Create a congenial atmosphere.

- Be accessible to team members.

- Provide reliable and accurate information.

- Use a win-win approach to solving problems.

3. Show the contribution of the team to overall organizational objectives

The task to be done is the priority — not your position. Each person, no matter how low or menial their job is, is a partner in getting the task done. Everyone on the team knows and shares the vision behind or reason for the task being done. The team members have shared aspirations, goals, dreams and attitudes.

Input is sought from every member of the group. People who contribute ideas, extra effort or time are acknowledged and appreciated.

You extend authority to trained team members. You coach and develop others on the job. You communicate up and down the corporate ladder.

4. Create commitment

A successful team is committed to itself and its members and to the company for which it works. You can't buy commitment, nor can you force it. Commitment comes from an individual decision, made by each team member, based on a sense of ownership of the team and of the job.

If you want a deeply committed team, you must supply five essential ingredients:

1. Meaningful work

2. Personal contribution

3. Community with other persons

4. Personal growth

5. Influence of each person

The Power of Delegation in Team Development

One of the best ways to build and develop your team is to develop skills in the art of delegation. Delegation is perhaps the most difficult task for the supervisor. You must learn that you are no longer a doer but a delegator.

You can't utilize the "If I work harder … " mentality. Your "doing everything" is not going to be effective. You need to work through the efforts of others to accomplish goals. You'll need to risk trusting subordinates to achieve. Letting go and depending on others to do a job that you are accountable for is difficult.

What Is Delegation?

*   It's the process of assigning certain tasks so that each person has a specific job to perform.

*   Delegation is granting authority to someone else to act and make decisions within prescribed limits.

*   Delegation is also creating a sense of responsibility in the person to perform the task adequately.

*   Delegation requires planning. The supervisor must decide what is to be done, who will do it, how to do it, how to direct it, how to establish standards of performance and how to measure results.

The Three D's of Delegation:

1. *Decide* what to delegate.

    - What needs to be done?

    - Who is qualified/skilled to do this job?

    - Who would benefit from learning how to do this job?

    - Is it a job that only I can do?

    - Do I have time to train a person to do this job?

2. *Don't* dump it all on one person.

    Beware the tendency to give more work to your high performers. It's a sad truth that those who get the work done only get more work to do.

3. *Do* give timely feedback on performance.

    - Explain standards of expectation and limits of authority.

    - Have a plan for directing or coaching if necessary.

    - Have a plan for regular, ongoing feedback.

The Vital People Skills for Team-Builders/Developers

Strengthen your team through:

- Encouraging them to grow as individuals

- Rewarding them for work well-done

- Fair arbitration of their disputes

- Seeking solutions to problems as they arise

- Actively listening

- Creating tolerant and tolerable working conditions

- Accepting input and ideas from everyone

- Communicating clearly

- Using guidelines rather than regulations

- Training and coaching for excellence

- Settling differences rather than stifling opposition

- Expanding the group to include others as necessary

- Leading by example, with mutual respect and motivation

Assess Your Team Leadership Skill Level

For each competency, rate yourself from 1-5.

1 — Need to improve

2 — Sometimes manage to do this, but room for improvement

3 — Can do this with some effort

4 — Do this in most cases

5 — Very skillful in this area

1. Achieve results by motivating and inspiring a winning team or work group _____

2. Establish and communicate a vision and future direction of the work unit _____

3. Set challenging standards of achievement _____

4. Articulate improvement opportunities in a way that builds commitment to common goals and energizes others to seek and implement solutions _____

5. Help team overcome the "pain" of change _____

6. Create a work environment characterized by participation/involvement and continuous learning/improvement _____

7. Allow individuals to collectively achieve their highest levels _____

Reflections

What are your greatest strengths as a team-builder?

How can you use these strengths to develop the areas in which you perceive a need to improve?

Team Leadership by Example

What kind of example do you set for your team? Answer these questions honestly.

1. How do you respond to emergencies? What is your reaction to a crisis?

2. How do you deal with outside pressures?

3. How do you respond to change?

4. Do you listen to new ideas?

5. Do you deal consistently with team members?

6. What kind of messages do you get from your superiors? How do they affect the way you lead your team?

11 PROBLEM-SOLVING AND DECISION-MAKING

What Is a Problem?

A problem is a gap between what is at this moment and what is desired in the future. A problem is something that is off-target or unwanted.

> Sharon, a production supervisor, recognized a problem when the 8 a.m. shift began and three workers were absent. The assembly line would be shut down if she didn't solve the problem quickly. What were her options? Call others in on overtime? Keep three over from the night shift? Set up for another product that required fewer workers?
>
> What were the trade-offs for Sharon? The first two options would result in extra labor costs. The third option would result in downtime to set up for the other product plus the downtime to shift back to the original product later.
>
> Which product was needed for filling outstanding orders? Which option would lose customers? Which was the priority?
>
> Sharon had options — lots of them. She needed to decide which was the best choice. Her decision was to keep three workers from the night shift and pay overtime.
>
> To implement her decision, she notified three workers to stay.

Your Job

Top-level managers see their subordinate managers and supervisors as individuals who are hired and paid to solve problems and make decisions. Of course, they may use other language, "stay on top of things," "keep within the budget," "improve morale," but they all boil down to the basics: identify and solve problems.

Few problems or performance discrepancies solve themselves. In fact, like leaky roofs or noisy engines, they can only get worse. Your job is to fix a problem before it gets worse.

Your frame of mind will have a great deal of impact on your problem-solving and decision-making. If you perceive the problem as a headache, you'll only apply limited enthusiasm and optimism to it. Conversely, if the problem is seen as a challenge with an opportunity for growth and innovation, you'll make a super effort to solve it.

> Gloria and Gail were both appointed supervisors at the same time. At lunch, they were comparing their new positions.
>
> "I sure inherited a lot of problems," moaned Gloria. "The production line has a lot of glitches, and it slows down our performance. And then, my top man, Bill, is threatening to quit if I don't do something about Miriam. They've got some kind of personality conflict going — it's turning into a feud, and everyone is taking sides. And just this morning, the boss came breathing down my neck to do something about quality control. It's just a big can of worms. I don't know how I'm going to handle it all."
>
> "I know what you mean," said Gail. "I've had a few surprises myself. I didn't know that our budget had been cut by 10 percent just before I came on. It's going to be interesting to see how we can still keep up production and make things work. And I've got three senior ladies who think they're on vacation, only they're still on the job. Somehow, I need to find a way to challenge them and light their fires again. As for my boss, she's always breathing down my

neck, too. I'll have to make sure she only sees good things happening. That'll look good on my next performance appraisal."

Which of these two new supervisors is likely to rise above the problems surrounding her? And which one is going to suffer the stress and strain of seemingly insurmountable problems?

The best advice anyone can give to a problem-solver is to expect adversity, not serenity. Although we might like the world to be neat, tidy, orderly and very predictable, the realities are that it is more likely to be murky, askew, pitfall-laden, and neither friendly nor controllable. So when the going gets tough and the problems mount up, it's a good idea to engage in a bit of positive self-talk. Try something like, "O.K., I've been hired to handle these problems. If there were no problems, there'd be no need to hire me."

Finally, as a manager, wrestling with problems is the heart of your job. You'll have to accept them as they come — easy or hard, fun or irritating, new or old, of your own doing or someone else's doing. Most of all, you have to take ownership of a problem. It may not be *your* fault — but it is *your* problem if it comes within the province of your job.

The Problem-Solving Model

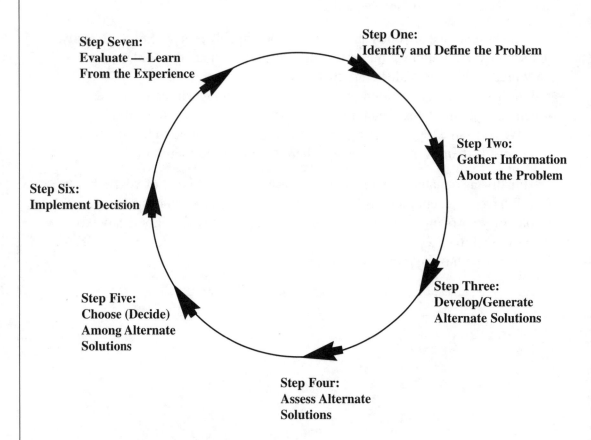

Step Seven:
Evaluate — Learn
From the Experience

Step One:
Identify and Define the Problem

Step Two:
Gather Information
About the Problem

Step Six:
Implement Decision

Step Three:
Develop/Generate
Alternate Solutions

Step Five:
Choose (Decide)
Among Alternate
Solutions

Step Four:
Assess Alternate
Solutions

Step One: Identify and Define the Problem

It's obvious that you can't solve a problem if you haven't identified it properly. What is the *real* issue? Sometimes in your haste to solve a problem, you may not have the time for a careful diagnosis.

Remember the new supervisor Gloria, who had a slowdown on the production line that she attributed to a glitch in the system? Poor Gloria. After spending endless, frustrating hours tracking down the glitches and fixing them, the line is still slow. Finally, weeks later, Gloria discovers that the problem is actually Miriam who is sabotaging Bill's efforts by deliberately bypassing quality control. The slow production is all part of their intradepartmental feud and has nothing to do with "glitches" at all.

The secret to identifying problems is to ask the right questions.

1. What is going on that tells you a problem exists? Which end results point to a problem?

2. Is it your problem? Why? If it's not your problem, why not? If it is your problem, who else (stakeholders) is involved?

3. What is the cost of not solving this problem? Is it small enough to merit not solving the problem?

4. How often does the problem occur? Is there a significant trend?

5. Where does the problem take place? Is it widespread or isolated?

6. Is there any relation to particular policies, procedures, rules, forms, processes?

7. Is it an equipment-related problem?

8. Are hazards or fatigue factors at work?

9. What remedial action, if any, has been considered? What actions, if any, have been applied already? With what results?

10. What end result would you like to have happen? How much change

is necessary to achieve that result — minimal or major?

Step Two: Gather Information About the Problem

If you want a high-quality solution to your problems, the solutions must be data-based. Unfortunately, the investment of time needed to collect the facts and information is not always an option for managers. For most managers, problem-solving means "putting out fires," not finding out how the fire started!

A common myth of problem-solving is that to solve the problem successfully, you must "gather the facts." But to assume that gathering facts is a certain route to solving a problem is too simplistic. You have to talk to people when getting the facts, and each person brings his own value system, background and perception to his version of the facts. You must ask:

- Whose facts?

- What facts?

- What is and is not relevant?

- How hard (quantifiable) or soft (qualitative) are these facts?

- To what degree do I accept opinion as fact?

- How current or recent is the data?

- Which sources are acceptable and which are not?

- When is enough data enough data?

Be careful not to fall into the trap of making causative assumptions when gathering the facts, that is, confusing the cause with the effect. If your begonia plant is turning yellow, then the problem — yellow leaves — is a symptom (effect) of a deeper cause. Low morale is not the problem — it is the symptom of a deeper cause. Absenteeism is not the problem — it is a symptom of something else. The task is to dig deeper to learn the precise causes.

Step Three: Develop/Generate Alternate Solutions

Too often, managers opt for immediate solutions rather than generate a large number of solutions to choose from. Brainstorming is one of the best means of generating ideas. A brainstorming session has five key ground rules:

1. "Freewheeling" is wanted.

2. "Hitchhiking" on an idea is OK.

3. Quantity is wanted.

4. Critical remarks are taboo.

5. Evaluation takes place after the session.

Step Four: Assess Alternate Solutions

If Step Three generates a large number of solutions to your problem, then you must be able to assess those solutions in order to make a high-quality selection. If you latch onto the first option you find, you may not choose the best possibility. Here are some ways for you to assess the solutions that you've generated:

1. **Voting**

    This can be done by a show of hands or vocally. When a problem is being solved by a group, this is the best method.

2. **Risk analysis**

    Set up four columns for each solution: Expectations, Concerns, Favorable Consequences, Unfavorable Consequences. When you've filled in the columns for each solution, rate them as to most likely and least likely to occur. Which solution has more likely opportunities than risks?

3. **Ranking with criteria**

    If you've ever interviewed candidates for a job, you'll probably be familiar with this technique. Basically, make a list of the criteria for a good solution to your problem. They could be: easy to implement, doesn't cost anything, doesn't eliminate staff positions, etc.

Then, give a ranking for each one. For example, 10 points for cost, 9 points for staff, etc. Add the total — that's the perfect solution figure.

Now, go through each of your solutions and assess them on the criteria ranking. For example, your first solution might be very expensive, so it would only get two points on the cost ranking.

When done, add up the totals for each solution. The closest total to the perfect solution figure is your optimum choice.

Step Five: Choose (Decide) Among Alternate Solutions

In Step Four, you learned how to assess the worth of alternate solutions generated in Step Three. Now "decision time" has arrived. You're ready to select one of the choices that you assessed highly. Make your decision based on these key elements:

- Values

- Overall view

- Cost

- Risk reduction

- Pilot runs

- Intuitive choice

Step Six: Implement Decision — Converting Hope Into Reality

To ensure that your plan proceeds in a systematic, orderly way, you need to consider these elements:

- What is to be done (activities, functions) in logical order or sequence

- Who is to do them (assume responsibility)

- When each step is to be started

- When each step is to be completed

- What resources are needed for each step

- The indicator of successful completion of each step

Step Seven: Evaluate — Did Your Plan Work?

Evaluation is comparing the results/outcomes with the goals/objectives. When you evaluate your decision, you must focus on measurable elements such as profitability, response/attitude, quality, costs, quality of work life, etc.

Evaluation should answer these questions:

1. Was the decision a proper one?

2. Did I consider enough options?

3. Was the implementation plan effective?

4. What did I learn from this problem-solving and decision-making endeavor?

5. If my decision was an appropriate one, what can I learn from this success?

6. Conversely, if the decision produced a less-than-successful result or experience, what can I learn from it?

What if things turned out less well than you expected? In our success-oriented culture, failure is something you don't like to dwell on. Yet, failure can be a great teacher. What is significant about failure is that it is inevitably part of your learning process. Remember — failure and defeat don't mean the same thing. Failure is simply an opportunity to decide what you can do better next time.

Problem-Solving and Decision-Making:
A Quiz to Encourage Reflection

Circle Y (Yes) or N (No) for each statement.

1. I follow a multistep problem-solving and
   decision-making model to ensure making a sound decision. **Y   N**

2. I try to make decisions on the basis of facts, reason
   and logic as opposed to relying on subjective factors. **Y   N**

3. I search for options (alternatives) before deciding on
   a single course of action. **Y   N**

4. I consider the importance of values — mine and those of
   others — underlying a decision before deciding. **Y   N**

5. When faced with a problem, I decide early on whether to
   solve it alone or involve others in the problem-solving process. **Y   N**

6. I understand that intuition can be used in decision-making
   if analytical methods are inadequate. **Y   N**

7. I recognize the importance of group wisdom in
   making decisions. **Y   N**

8. I am interested in making high-quality rather than quick
   decisions, so I encourage expression of divergent views
   by my team. **Y   N**

9. I realize that I cannot make decisions in cocoon fashion,
   that I must consider how they might look to and impact
   the rest of my organization. **Y   N**

Reflections

10. I also consider whether my decisions might have a ripple effect outside of my department. **Y   N**

11. I recognize that every decision entails risk. I try to assess possible consequences and make plans to minimize them. **Y   N**

12. I avoid delaying decisions or hoping that something might happen to get me off the hook. **Y   N**

13. I consider the factors (need for action) and timing (when to decide and implement) of a decision. **Y   N**

14. I try to make my decisions on a cost-effective basis. **Y   N**

15. My decision-making stands the tests of ethics. **Y   N**

16. Our team discussions end up with firm decisions, definite plans for action, and fixed responsibility and procedures. **Y   N**

Scoring

Give yourself 5 points for each "Yes" answer.

• 70-80 points: Decision-making is one of your strong skills.

• 59-69 points: You understand the key concepts of this skill area quite well. Your main need is to zero in on the added opportunities for growth that you've identified.

• Below 59 points: You have a lot of work to do — serious self-assessment and behavior change — to grow your skills in problem-solving and decision-making.

Reflections

12 POLITICAL SAVVY

You can't ignore the political system. The political aspects of organizations are inherently tied to the informal organization, your personal power and influence and the old-boy network. A manager must be skilled at influencing, compromising and collaborating in order to achieve personal, departmental and organizational goals. You'll need to learn how to develop the network of mutual obligations with others. You may need to build coalitions to gain support for decisions or activities you're engaged in. You need to develop your personal power of influence to be effective personally and professionally. Getting into the network helps you and your department become more effective and productive.

A real dilemma for many women is that building power, political connections, informal networks and coalitions is not a familiar activity. Many women lack experience in these areas.

Developing Interpersonal Power

Interpersonal power refers to the power you possess as others perceive it. Personal power fits into five main categories:

1. **Reward/punishment:** Your ability to provide meaningful rewards or to mete out effective punishment.

2. **Position/role:** The power that is inherent in your position in the organization or your role in relation to another person.

3. **Skills/expertise:** Your professional skills, technical skills, managerial skills, social skills or any type of skill that is useful to or respected by others.

4. **Information/data:** Your access to facts, figures, gossip, any information that another considers necessary, helpful or interesting and that is not readily available anywhere else.

5. **Charisma/identification:** The extent to which another is personally attracted to you and is able to identify with you.

Establishing a Support Network

Building networks of mutual obligations with others is the name of the game. Your support network consists of the relationships you've established, both inside and outside the company, that are based on mutual goodwill, trust and willingness to help. They are business friendships that are mutually supportive.

Your support network functions as your power base, which means it is an essential source of power to you.

Use the Informal Organization

Management is not an individual sport — managing is the process of utilizing people from the informal and formal organization to accomplish goals. It's a team attitude — you need others not only for goal accomplishment, but for support, guidance, direction and advice. You'll need to tap into the political, informal networking system and learn appropriate behaviors if you want advancement and to be effective for your organization.

The informal organization is that network of people that you won't find on the organizational chart — but it's where the real action is.

> Marcie's department works closely with Joe's department. Marcie and Joe are on the same "line" of the organizational chart. However, Marcie has learned that while Joe may be the official supervisor and

have the supervisory position, Karen, a staff person in Joe's department, has the real power to get things done. In other words, Joe has the positional power, but Karen may have the reward power or influence base. Marcie keeps Joe informed and makes sure he knows what is happening, but it's Karen she goes to when she wants to get things done. Marcie makes sure that she and Karen are part of an informal network of mutual obligation. If they weren't, Karen wouldn't be so likely to make sure that things happen for Marcie's department.

How do you learn how to use the informal organization and establish a reciprocal network for you and your department?

1. Move around the organization. Look for groups that can provide your department with needed resources.

2. Become acquainted with these groups.

3. Never let a chance go by. Always indicate your appreciation of something a group did for you.

4. Conduct yourself in a friendly, professional and confident manner.

5. Look for signals. Look for indications of informal leadership or power. The effective manager utilizes the informal network.

Getting Into the Old-Boy Network

We all know how the old-boy network operates. A promotion is open within the organization. The network talks about who would be most suitable — usually one of their own. With a minimum of fuss and paperwork, the person is appointed to the new position, and you're left wondering why you didn't know the position was available or why you weren't considered for it.

Some women complain bitterly how they are blocked from this network. They aren't invited to the formal or informal social functions. Many women have reported that it isn't necessarily the physical exclusion from the interaction with the network that hinders their advancement, but the lack of information they receive. The network has what they need — who's doing what, what plans are in the making, what decisions are being considered, etc. *Information is influence* and getting it is powerful.

Eight Ways to Be Included in the Old-Boy Network

1. Demonstrate self-confidence and initiative.

2. Acquire the behaviors and traits of successful managers (i.e., savvy of the informal organization, ability to see the big picture, being a direct communicator, having a high profile).

3. Know your organization from top to bottom (how it works, how things get done, how it's organized, strategic plans, etc.).

4. Personally meet as many of the movers and shakers as you can.

5. Establish multiple reciprocal networks with others.

6. Get psychological support from informal women's groups, both inside and outside the organization.

7. Get involved in high-profile activities — high-visibility projects, task forces, etc.

8. Become indispensable for the success of key projects (i.e., you're an invaluable planner or organizer, you have network contacts, you have good people skills, you can motivate others, etc.).

Working With a Mentor

In most organizations, entrance to middle- and top-management echelons is not determined by mere competence. It's not *what* you know, but *who* you know. Virtually all people who make it to the top have at least one mentor or sponsor from this powerful, influential group.

Locating Potential Mentors

1. Identify powerful, secure, upwardly mobile people in your organization who are respected and have influence.

2. Figure out ways to become acquainted with them.

3. Seek their advice. Ask intelligent, thoughtful questions. (Warning: avoid acting helpless.)

4. Ask for further support if the relationship goes well.

5. Communicate that you are fully committed to achieving your goals. (This is especially important with a male mentor because some men still believe that a woman holds her career as a secondary concern.)

Handling Political Games

Estimates show that nearly 75 percent of managers who are forced out of their jobs fail because of organizational politics. When you move into a leadership job, you must assess your political savvy if you want to survive.

The extent to which you become involved in the politics of the organization depends upon your attitude toward people and your personal power. Generally, if you respect people and are direct and honest with them, they are most likely to respond in kind. But, if you initiate "dirty" tactics, play political games, backstab or sabotage others, you can expect the same kind of treatment.

You'll need to create your own strategies for a positive game plan. Here are five tips:

1. Look for the cause. Why did someone act the way she did? Was it really a game or a true misunderstanding?

2. Don't take it personally. Usually you're not the only target for a political game — anyone is open for a shot. Don't assume that there's something wrong with you — they're just trying to figure out how to pull your strings.

3. Stay goal-oriented. In each political situation, ask yourself, "How will this affect my professional goals?" Respond based on your answer.

4. Develop a support network and use it. Ask for supportive action where it will do the most good and look for an opportunity to return the favor.

5. Document transactions. These will be invaluable in backing up your case in your need to confront a player's game.

Just remember that women like you who are moving into leadership roles will encounter a variety of experiences in the workplace for which they haven't been trained or prepared. The task is to gain that knowledge and experience in as many ways as possible — books, tapes, conferences, seminars, classes, networking and workshops. Never allow yourself to become complacent with your current skill level but become instead a lifelong learner, committed to acquiring ongoing knowledge and expertise.

Finding a Mentor

1. Who is one person in the organization who would be an effective mentor for me?

2. What knowledge and skills can I gain from this person?

3. What are some ways in which I could meet this person?

4. What committees, task forces or groups is this person involved in? Can I also get involved in them? How?

5. What is one way I could approach this person to ask for advice?

Reflections

Do You Have the Profile of a Typical Leader?

1. An achieving person.
    List three things you have achieved in your organization.

2. An identification with a field or profession.
    What is your particular field or profession?

3. A high degree of individuality but relates well to people.
    How are you different from the rest? What makes you stand out?
    What are your particular people skills?

4. A strong sense of self-esteem and respect for others' individuality.
    How do you feel about your role as a leader?

5. A high level of motivation and achievement.
    What motivates you to move into management?

Reflections

Reflections

INDEX

NOTES

NOTES

NOTES

Buy any 3, get 1 FREE!

Get a 60-Minute Training Series™ Handbook FREE ($14.95 value)* when you buy any three. See back of order form for full selection of titles.

These are helpful how-to books for you, your employees and co-workers. Add to your library. Use for new-employee training, brown-bag seminars, promotion gifts and more. Choose from many popular titles on a variety of lifestyle, communication, productivity and leadership topics. Exclusively from National Press Publications.

DESKTOP HANDBOOK ORDER FORM

Ordering is easy:

1. Complete both sides of this Order Form, detach, and mail, fax or phone your order to:

    Mail: National Press Publications
    P.O. Box 419107
    Kansas City, MO 64141-6107

    Fax: 1-913-432-0824
    Phone: 1-800-258-7248 (in Canada 1-800-685-4142)
    Internet: http://www.natsem.com/books.html

2. Please print:

Name_____ Position/Title _____

Company/Organization_____

Address_____City _____

State/Province_____ZIP/Postal Code _____

Telephone (____)_____ Fax (____) _____

3. Easy payment:

❑   Enclosed is my check or money order for $_____ (total from back).
    Please make payable to National Press Publications.

Please charge to:
❑   MasterCard   ❑   VISA   ❑   American Express

Credit Card No. _____ Exp. Date_____

Signature_____

● ●
MORE WAYS TO SAVE:

SAVE 33%!!! BUY 20-50 COPIES of any title ... pay just $9.95 each ($11.25 Canadian).

SAVE 40%!!! BUY 51 COPIES OR MORE of any title ... pay just $8.95 each ($10.25 Canadian).

* $17.00 in Canada

Buy 3, get 1 FREE!
60-MINUTE TRAINING SERIES™ HANDBOOKS

TITLE	RETAIL PRICE	QTY	TOTAL
8 Steps for Highly Effective Negotiations #424	$14.95		
Assertiveness #4422	$14.95		
Balancing Career and Family #415	$14.95		
Delegate for Results #4592	$14.95		
Dynamic Communication Skills for Women #413	$14.95		
Exceptional Customer Service #4882	$14.95		
Fear & Anger: Slay the Dragons… #4302	$14.95		
Getting Things Done #4112	$14.95		
How to Coach an Effective Team #4308	$14.95		
How to De-Junk Your Life #4306	$14.95		
How to Handle Conflict and Confrontation #4952	$14.95		
How to Manage Your Boss #493	$14.95		
How to Supervise People #4102	$14.95		
How to Work with People #4032	$14.95		
Inspire & Motivate Through Performance Reviews #4232	$14.95		
Listen Up: Hear What's Really Being Said #4172	$14.95		
Motivation and Goal-Setting #4962	$14.95		
A New Attitude #4432	$14.95		
Parenting: Ward & June… #486	$14.95		
The Polished Professional #426	$14.95		
The Power of Innovative Thinking #428	$14.95		
The Power of Self-Managed Teams #4222	$14.95		
Powerful Communication Skills #4132	$14.95		
Present with Confidence #4612	$14.95		
The Secret to Developing Peak Performers #4692	$14.95		
Self-Esteem: The Power to Be Your Best #4642	$14.95		
Shortcuts to Organized Files & Records #4307	$14.95		
The Stress Management Handbook #4842	$14.95		
Supreme Teams: How to Make Teams Work #4303	$14.95		
Techniques to Improve Your Writing Skills #460	$14.95		
Thriving on Change #4212	$14.95		
Women and Leadership #4632	$14.95		
The Write Stuff #414	$14.95		

Sales Tax All purchases subject to state and local sales tax. Questions? Call **1-800-258-7248**		
Subtotal		$
Add 7% Sales Tax *(Or add appropriate state and local tax)*		$
Shipping and Handling *($3 one item; 50¢ each additional item)*		$
TOTAL		$

VIP No. 922-008438-099   5/00